Escaping Daddy

Escaping Daddy

A heartbreaking true story of a brave little girl

MARIA LANDON

with Andrew Crofts

HARPER
element

This is a work of non-fiction. In order to protect privacy, some names and places have been changed.

HarperElement
An Imprint of HarperCollins*Publishers*
77–85 Fulham Palace Road,
Hammersmith, London W6 8JB

www.harpercollins.co.uk

and *HarperElement* are trademarks
of HarperCollins*Publishers* Ltd

First published by HarperElement 2009

4

© 2009 Maria Landon

Maria Landon asserts the moral right to
be identified as the author of this work

A catalogue record of this book is
available from the British Library

ISBN 978-0-00-726883-2

Printed and bound in Great Britain by
Clays Ltd, St Ives plc

Mixed Sources
Product group from well-managed forests and other controlled sources
www.fsc.org Cert no. SW-COC-1806
© 1996 Forest Stewardship Council

FSC is a non-profit international organization established to promote the responsible management of the world's forests. Products carrying the FSC label are independently certified to assure consumers that they come from forests that are managed to meet the social, economic and ecological needs of present and future generations.

Find out more about HarperCollins and the environment at
www.harpercollins.co.uk/green

For the true heroes of this story,
Brendan and Thomas

xx

'It's never too late to have a happy childhood'
Tom Robbins

Escaping
Daddy

Foreword

'Get that down you,' Dad said, handing me a vodka and lime.

I took a big gulp and shuddered as it burned my throat. My hand shook as I applied eyeliner in thick black strokes. I was just thirteen years old and getting myself ready for a night working on the Block, the section of Ber Street in Norwich where men cruised in their cars looking for sex.

'Hurry up!' Dad growled. 'The sooner you get started, the sooner it'll be over.'

I took another big swig and the alcohol made me dizzy but didn't relieve the sheer terror about what lay ahead. Every time I got into a strange man's car I knew I could be robbed, beaten up, or worse. It never got any easier.

Dad gripped my elbow and led me out onto the street. I was teetering in my ridiculously high heels, stumbling with fear, trying to make my mind go blank. *Just do it, just get through it*, I was thinking. *There's no way out.*

There were other girls working the same patch and they eyed me with suspicion and hostility as I arrived in their territory. None of them said anything while Dad was around because they all knew what he was like. I was by far the youngest one out there, but none of the customers were going to complain about that.

When the time came and a car pulled up, I couldn't bring myself to actually walk forward and talk to the driver. My heart was beating so hard I thought I was going to faint. Dad stepped out of the shadows behind me and pushed me towards the road.

'Get out there now,' he hissed. 'Go and earn your keep.'

I knew from experience that he wasn't going to change his mind and let me go home now. I had no choice but to go through with it.

'Do you want business?' I asked the next driver through the open window, my voice not much more than a whisper.

He did. Terms were agreed and I got into the car under Dad's watchful eye, then we drew away from the others into the darkness.

Working on the Block was a regular part of my life between the ages of thirteen and fifteen but never something I got used to. I always hated it but I didn't think I deserved any better. It was my destiny to provide men with what they wanted and to be controlled by Dad. That's all I was good for, as he had told me over and over again throughout my childhood.

So when I started trying to break away from Dad's influence and form adult relationships with men, I didn't have a clue how they should work. I thought I needed a man to protect me in the world, and in return I had to provide him with sex and do as he told me. Was that what other women did? Was that how the world worked? Wasn't it?

'No one else will ever love you, Ria,' my dad would always tell me, 'not the way I do. I'm the only one who will ever truly love you.'

I still believed those words long after I should have been grown-up enough to know better. Everyone wants to believe what their parents tell them, don't they?

Even when I stopped having anything to do with Dad, the lessons he had taught me rang in my ears. There was an invisible chord still linking us no matter how hard I tried to pull away. What hope could I have of ever being happy? What would it take?

Chapter One

Childhood

Right from the beginning Dad would say I was his favourite child, and that would make me very proud. He was big and handsome and always seemed heroic to me because he was so popular and flamboyant, always the centre of attention wherever he went. Everyone loved my tall, dark, handsome dad. He had a powerful presence, always immaculately turned out in a suit and tie and known for being good company, never able to resist playing up to an adoring crowd of admirers. He was so plausible he could tell people anything and get away with it. He cultivated an image for himself as a lovable local rogue and 'a bit of a character', but as well as being a charmer he was a bully and a show-off and he had an uncontrollable temper, which frequently spilled over into violence.

I always wanted to please him, to obey him, to win his approval and to avoid getting a beating. But the more I yearned for his approval the more he would withhold it, telling me how worthless and fat and ugly I was, and I continued to believe him even when I could clearly see the sort of man he truly was beneath the superficial bravado. My father was a pimp and a drunk and had been all his adult life.

His total possession of me started on the morning I was born, when I'm told that he paraded boastfully around the hospital, completely drunk, puffing on a cigar and joking that he was going to make me 'the best little prostitute on the block'. Except he wasn't joking; he was deadly serious.

'Pity I haven't got four girls,' he would tell anyone who would listen, 'because then I could run a proper little brothel and never work again.'

To him these weren't such shocking announcements because that was the world he lived in, the world he sought to control in any way he could and the world I grew up in. He truly believed that all women were 'sitting on a goldmine' and that they were mad if they didn't exploit it to their own advantage, and if possible to his advantage as well. He never held down a proper job in all the years I knew him, drinking away whatever money he could bully the women in his life into earning for him by selling their bodies on the streets, combined with whatever welfare payments he could blag.

Despite the fact he always swore that my mum was the love of his life, just as she would swear that he was the love of hers, he had even nagged and bullied her into selling her body to passing kerb-crawlers in order to provide him with drinking money. Such behaviour seemed normal to him because all the friends that he spent his days and nights with were the same: either alcoholics or hookers, or both. I was too young to be able to remember the years when Mum and Dad were together, but I can imagine how it was from what they and other people have told me, and from the way he went on to treat me and everyone else. Despite the fact that he worshipped Mum, he still undermined her confidence at every possible opportunity, one minute telling her how gorgeous she was and the next telling her she was ugly and useless. He would beat and kick her ruthlessly when she tried to stand up to him, determined to break her spirit and make her obedient. When she finally decided she had had enough and left us when I was six years old, he spent the rest of his life telling everyone how brokenhearted he was, and threatening to kill himself whenever he was drunk.

It was the same technique he used to manipulate and control everyone in his life. Dad had a way of making people do what he wanted with a mixture of charm, violent bullying and manipulation. He dominated and terrorised Mum in the same way as he would later dominate and terrorise us. The fact that she had borne him four children made no difference to the way he treated her or the things he expected her to do for him.

My brother Terry was the first to be born from their great teenage love affair and I came along a year later in 1966. It seems Dad was willing to tolerate our existence, although he still enjoyed hurting and frightening us whenever the mood took him, but by the time our brothers, Chris and Glen, came along in 1969 and 1970 he had lost all patience with the demands of small children. He was so violent towards the two babies Mum didn't dare bring them out of their bedroom when he was around and, as she slipped into a pit of depression herself, they gradually became forgotten for longer and longer periods, remaining silent and fearful behind that closed bedroom door.

I was only little but I remember glancing at that door, hearing the whimpering noises behind it and smelling the awful, eye-watering smell of their unchanged nappies, a smell that permeated through the upper floor of the house. Mum only dared to bring them out to feed and change them when Dad had gone out somewhere, and they were pitiful creatures: very thin, with scratches and sores all over their skin, and huge staring eyes. I felt desperately sorry, and guilty that I was allowed to come downstairs and eat meals with the family while they weren't – but what could I do about it? I was just too young to help them.

Dad managed to convince Mum that she would only have to turn tricks once or twice, that he was just asking her to do him a favour because he was skint and they both needed some drinking money, but it wasn't long before she realised she was being naïve and that the more she earned for him the harder he would make her work. Dad had realised that pimping was the easiest way imaginable for him to earn money. However much she might have loved him, there was a point beyond which even she wasn't willing to put up with him any more.

Mum finally gave up hope of anything ever changing and had a nervous breakdown, walking away from all of us without even saying goodbye. I have only the dimmest of memories of a time when she was there with us and I have no picture of her leaving. All I can really remember is me and Dad and Terry on our own together and being told that she had gone. She left us all, including Chris and Glen, still festering in their locked bedroom. Dad couldn't believe that he had lost the love of his life and his drinking grew steadily worse, increasing the lake of self-pity he chose to wallow in. I think he was genuinely shocked that she'd gone, but he was also upset at losing the money she had brought in.

As soon as she could, Mum alerted social services to the danger we were all in now that we were alone with Dad. When social workers came round they found Chris and Glen shut in their bedroom in a terrible state. They were two and three years old, staring straight ahead with deadened eyes. Chris was rocking rhythmically back and forth in his cot and Glen was so hungry he was actually eating the contents of his own soiled nappy. Dad told everyone who would listen that Mum was the villain of the piece for leaving her children in such a state and he was able to make out that he was the innocent victim of her cold heart just as much as we were. Chris and Glen were both put into a foster home while Terry and I were left with Dad, who was busy boasting how he was going to bring us up on his own, thus winning the sympathy of all his women friends in the pub.

'Poor old Terry. His wife's up and left him and he's doing his best to be a good dad to the little ones,' they'd say, oblivious to the fact that he didn't look after us at all. It fell to me to get meals for us, try to clean our clothes and get us to school on time, while Dad was out cavorting with his girlfriends or staying up all night drinking.

Once Mum had gone we never heard from her again for eight years. We didn't hear from our grandparents or any of our other relatives either. Somehow Dad managed to intimidate them all into staying away, just as he intimidated Terry and me into obeying his every order with the beatings and the hours we spent locked in the windowless coal cellar if we displeased him. We never even received any birthday or Christmas cards from other family members. It seemed he was right when he told us the whole world had forgotten we existed and he was the only person we could rely on to care about us and look after us.

'I'm the only person you can trust,' he kept saying. 'I'm the only person who will ever love you.'

With Mum gone he turned the full force of his pain, anger and misery onto us, while to the rest of the world he remained the jovial life and soul of the party, the hero whose feckless wife had deserted him and who was struggling to bring up the kids on his own. In the privacy of the house he did everything he could to make sure we were his devoted slaves, particularly me, playing endless mind games to make sure I would stay loyal and obedient and crushed.

'You're fat and ugly,' he would tell me all the time, 'no one will ever love you except me. Even your own mother left you.'

I was convinced it was all true. Sometimes he would cuddle me and then push me away for no reason. He would tell Terry that he had been Mum's 'favourite', making it all the worse that she had deserted him, and making me feel all the worse for not being as good as my brother. He certainly didn't bother about our clothes or any other aspects of our care. I got a letter home from the headmistress of my school, suggesting that it would be a good idea to 'clean Maria up' but Dad countered with such a string of expletives that the poor woman never dared to follow through with a face-to-face meeting.

I wished Dad wouldn't treat Terry and me so badly, but I still adored him and was still desperate to please him in any way I could, following him around like a faithful little puppy. All his days were spent in the pubs and the bookies, with us waiting outside in the cold for him to stumble back out, while his nights were spent drinking and playing cards with his friends. Sometimes he would force us to join in till the early hours of the morning; other times we would be sent upstairs and threatened with dire consequences if we even came out to use the toilet. He would make us go shoplifting, mainly to steal whisky for him and his friends, and he even had us cashing stolen giros at one stage.

Dad couldn't read so I always had to read things out for him. By the time I was eight or nine he had started making me read to him from his pornographic magazines while he masturbated. I didn't understand what he was doing but I knew it felt wrong and weird. I had no choice, though, because if I refused I'd get beaten with a stick or with his slipper. Then he began to make me lie beside him so he could slide his fingers inside my pants, which I hated. He said he would teach me everything I needed to know, but if I ever told anyone about what he did I'd be sent away to live in a children's home full of perverts who would torture and rape me. It sounded terrifying and I begged him not to make me go there.

His sexual demands didn't stop at touching me.

'Do you want a lollipop?' he asked one evening when he got in from the pub.

'Yes please, Daddy,' I said, confused as he marched me upstairs and started masturbating in front of me.

'Do you want a lollipop, then?' he asked again.

'Yes. Where are they?'

12

'Come here,' he said and as I leaned across he grabbed my head. 'Suck this!'

I felt as though I was suffocating and I struggled to get away, which made him angry. Tears were streaming down my face and I was gagging and choking, certain he was going to kill me. I couldn't breathe because his thing was so huge. It was a nightmare that never seemed to end.

Soon he was forcing me to take his penis in my mouth regularly and then he began trying to have penetrative sex with me, not caring how much he hurt or frightened or disgusted me, making it clear that there was no point struggling because it was going to happen anyway and I would just make it harder for myself by fighting. It hurt so much that I was convinced I was going to die. I thought I was being torn in half, but there was no point in struggling because he was too big and strong. He told me over and over that I must never tell anyone about the things we did together, terrifying me with stories of what would happen if I did.

'If I go to prison you and Terry will be sent to a children's home and everyone will hate you,' he would warn. 'You need to have your daddy here to protect you. This is our secret. No one will believe anything you say until you are ten anyway.'

I hated the things he did to me, but I still adored him and longed to please him so that he would stop hurting me and telling me how bad I was. I longed for the times when he was nice to me and told me I was his favourite. I'd do just about anything to win his praise. He was my dad and I loved him.

When I was twelve he took me up to the streets where the city's hookers plied their trade to kerb-crawlers. This was his little kingdom where he set himself up as a pimp, the place where everyone knew who he was. I knew a lot of the girls already because they often came round our house after they had been beaten up or robbed, looking on Dad as a friend and someone who understood their world because he was a part of it. Some of them were really good to me and I considered them to be my friends too. He proudly showed me where he had put Mum to work and where he was going to make me follow in her footsteps, spending my evenings lurking in the shadows as a steady stream of punters slowed down in their cars, in search of business, taking a look at the goods on offer.

I liked it the first time Dad got his friend Lucy to dress me up in a tight skirt and stilettos. I felt glamorous, like a little girl playing make-believe, and I was happy when Dad admired my legs and said they were just like Mum's. I didn't let myself think about working on the streets though. I hated what Dad did to me in his bed and couldn't bear to think about any other man doing it to me. My throat closed up in dread every time he talked about me becoming the best little prostitute on the Block.

But when I was thirteen, the day came when Dad decided I was ready to start fulfilling the destiny he had chosen for me. I felt an overwhelming sense of hopelessness as I got ready, knowing there was no way out of it so I might as well get it over with, just as he had told me a hundred times when he raped me. I obeyed him automatically, like a robot, still wanting to please him and win his love despite everything he had done to me. I had to drink a lot of vodka to build up my courage before the first time I went out on the street but I got through it somehow, trying to make my mind go blank as I spread my legs and let businessmen thrust away inside me.

Once I had serviced a few punters and earned him some money, Dad bought a bottle of whisky and took me back to Lucy's house to celebrate. The mix of whisky and vodka was too much for my young stomach and I threw up all over Dad's suit. I thought he would be angry but he wasn't – he just thought the whole thing was funny and in a way I was glad that I had been able to make him happy. But I dreaded having to work on the Block again. No matter how many times I did it, I always felt terrified as the car pulled off with me inside, and I always felt as though I had been raped afterwards, even though I was clutching the punter's money.

All the **girls** would use drink and drugs to help them get over their fears every time they went out on the street, or to drown out the memories afterwards. The irony was that once they had habits, they needed to go out to work more often in order to earn the money they needed to satisfy their cravings, creating vicious cycles that many never escaped from. I was no different to the rest and Dad was always happy to supply me with as much drink as it took to make me co-operative. He didn't approve of drugs, but there were plenty of other people around who were happy to supply me with those when I asked. I started on cannabis but before long speed became my drug of choice and I took it whenever I could get my hands on some.

There were times when Dad would get caught by the police for thieving or fighting and sent to prison for a while. Terry and I would then go into children's homes or foster homes and I was surprised to find that they weren't as terrible as Dad had warned me they would be. But by that time he had messed with my head so much that I couldn't settle anywhere. A lot of teachers and social workers told me that they thought I had the potential for a better life, but I always ended up back in trouble one way or another. As soon as he came out of prison Dad would order us to go back to him and I always wanted to go, hoping beyond hope that things would be different this time; that this time he would be kind to me, that he would stop doing those things to me.

But it was all a game to him. He convinced me that wherever I was taken I should run away and go back to him at the first opportunity. I never questioned this wisdom, even though I sometimes knew I was better off in the places the social workers sent me to. I desperately wanted us to be a happy little family, but he just wanted to have me in his power in the same way he had with Mum. Whatever efforts the authorities made to get me to safety he just had to snap his fingers and I would go running back to him. Sometimes I would try to explain to people what he was doing to me, but Dad always managed to get out of it, to turn everything round so it seemed as if I was the problem, not him.

Social workers were as confused as I was. One wrote about me: 'Maria is in some ways functioning at a four- or five-year-old level and in others at a sixteen-year-old level, plus being an intelligent twelve-year-old. She is over-fond of her dad and wants him close to her, up to a certain point, and beyond that she starts complaining.'

At one of the homes, when I was fourteen, I asked if they would try to make contact with Mum for us. They managed to track her down and she actually came to see us. For a while it looked as though Terry and I might be able to live with her, but we were all too damaged. Within six weeks the relationship had broken down because Mum couldn't cope with our disruptive behaviour and we were taken back into care.

I was fifteen and on the run from one of the care homes I'd been assigned to when I met a guy called Brian. He was a thirty-five-year-old biker and I fell in love with him because he was a kind and decent man. I had 'property of Brian' tattooed on my upper arm, just above a tattoo I already had of Dad's name. We even bought a silver ring down the market and announced to the world that we were in love. Brian gave me the courage to break away a little from Dad, even though I was still working on the street to make the money I needed for the drink and drugs I was using.

Brian wanted to help me to escape from my fear of Dad and from the social workers who he thought were letting me down, so we hitchhiked down to London together. It was a dream that neither of us had thought through and we ran out of money almost immediately. Brian might have been older than me but he wasn't capable of earning a wage and supporting us; he was a dreamer with a dope habit who liked playing his guitar. The only way we could support ourselves was for me to go back to work doing the one thing I knew how on the streets of King's Cross. I was terrified and I didn't want to do it, but the thought of going back to Norwich and letting Dad know I had failed was worse. I didn't want him to see that he had been right, that I couldn't manage without him.

The other prostitutes working in King's Cross all looked older and harder and more vicious than any of the girls I had ever met in Norwich. These were people who everyone had given up on, junkies and schizophrenics and God alone knew what else. I'd never really known many black people before and I didn't understand the way they or their pimps acted or talked to me. It was like occupying an alien landscape and everything seemed strange and dangerous, angry and aggressive. Most of the time I got myself high on speed or acid before I went out to work, just so that I could overcome my fears.

When the police eventually caught up with us they arrested Brian and Dad, accusing them both of living off my immoral earnings. Everyone knew Dad was a pimp but I was forced to stand in the witness box for an hour and half with him staring long and hard at me as I finally plucked up the courage to give evidence against him. Even then I still hated and loved him in equal proportions. I was relieved that people now believed me and that he was going to have to pay for what he had done to me over the years, but I also felt guilty that I was betraying him and ensuring he went back to prison again.

Everyone, including the judge, could see that Brian was my boyfriend and not a paedophile in the way Dad was, but he had still broken the law by sleeping with me while I was underage and so he had to serve six months in jail while Dad was given four years.

I don't think anyone in social services thought that I would wait for Brian, but I did, putting all my energies into finding new ways to escape from the care homes they put me in. Eventually, once Brian was free and I was seventeen, they admitted defeat and let us live together in Brian's council flat, which was the moment when I fell pregnant with his child.

I desperately wanted a child, having already suffered a miscarriage the previous year. Most of all I wanted to be a good mother. I wanted my baby to have the best possible start in life and never be made to feel the way I had felt throughout my childhood. As the date of the birth drew closer my intentions became more and more serious and I began to realise that Brian was never going to be able to be a good and responsible father. He might be a lovely, kind man, but he would never hold down a proper job and I could see that his drink and drug problems were getting worse not better. Dad would soon be out of prison and I was terrified of being forced back into his clutches simply because I had no alternative. I didn't want him to be allowed anywhere near my baby when it arrived.

I had wanted so much to be independent and to show the world, and Dad, that I was an adult and could manage on my own, but I realised the relationship with Brian wasn't going to work and I was going to have to throw myself on the mercy of the social services. I needed help. I hated the idea of people seeing me as a failure again and I was terrified they would insist on taking the baby away from me, but they responded graciously to my plea and eventually put me into a little flat on my own. So many people in the social services over the years had told me that they thought I could do better with my life, but I had never believed them, always allowing Dad's words to undermine my confidence and make me suspicious of anyone who told me I was better than I thought, that I could make something of my life if I wanted to.

My baby, Brendan, was the most wonderful thing that had ever happened to me. I didn't sleep at all the first night after his birth, just lying there staring at him, promising him I would do everything I possibly could to give him a decent life and that I would make sure he didn't have to endure the sort of upbringing I'd been given. I convinced myself that just because Mum had left us and Dad had abused me and put me on the streets didn't necessarily mean I was doomed to repeat all their mistakes. I told myself that by having such a wonderful baby to look after I would be one of the damaged children who managed to escape from their past. I had imagined that Dad was the only problem, not realising there would be other people and emotions lying in wait to ambush me.

In the euphoria of the first few hours with my baby I thought my problems were behind me – but they weren't. I was eighteen years old but inside the tense, feisty teenager I had become I was still a sad, desperate child. Despite the aggressive, cheeky face I showed to the outside world, I was feeling as lost and alone in the world as I had when my father first raped me and then laughed at my pain, terrified now that the shadows of my past would catch up with me again, dragging me back into his world of scams, populated as it always was by hookers, addicts and drunks.

Chapter Two

The Overdose

When I was a little girl, if anyone had asked what I wanted to do with my life I would have told them, 'I want to get married and have four children'. I guess that was because Mum and Dad had had four of us and I wanted to make up for all the mistakes they had made, do everything completely differently to the way they had. Perhaps I was hoping to get a childhood for myself through my own children. As I hadn't been able to do all those great parent/child things when I was the child, at least I would be able to do them as a mum.

But the reality was that after Brendan's birth I was lonely and broke, and insecure about my parenting skills. I didn't even seem to be able to make enough money to keep my new baby warm and safe without having to resort to shoplifting. I can still remember the sick feeling of guilt I experienced when I was caught stealing some bedding from a department store in Norwich. I had

Brendan with me at the time and when they took me up to the police station I dissolved into helpless sobbing and hysteria because I thought they were going to take him away from me.

I was never a good shoplifter, although I was a lot better than my brother Terry in the days when we were both small and Dad used to send us out every day to steal his whisky or some food for our supper. Whereas Dad seemed to see nothing wrong in stealing at all, as though it was just a fact of life that we had to get used to, I always felt guilty and tried to wriggle out of it. I stole an eyeliner pencil for myself once and felt so bad about it I took it back the next day. I was even more scared of being caught returning it than I had been when I originally slid it into my pocket.

The fact that I was having to turn to shoplifting again in order to provide for my baby made me feel like even more of a failure, as though I was fulfilling all Dad's worst predictions about how my future would be without him. However much I hated the way things were going, however, I also couldn't see any way I would ever be able to turn my life round and make everything decent. Once you have become part of that world of thieving and drinking and prostitution, especially when it is all you have ever known or had experience of, it is very hard to break out.

Although I was physically safe in my tiny flat, and was no longer being forced to climb into cars with strange men, inside I still felt like the same little girl whose father had decided on the day of her birth to turn her into a street walker. Even though I loved my baby, Brendan, more than anything or anyone I often found the pain of living too much to bear.

Apart from Brendan I had no family to turn to for comfort as the empty hours ticked by in that lonely little flat. Mum was living locally and I could telephone her whenever I wanted but she might as well have been at the other end of the country for all the help she was able to give me. I used to go to see her once a week for a few months after Brendan was born but her new partner had made it clear that he wanted nothing to do with her children from the past so I could only visit when he was out at work. When she saw me struggling to cope it must have brought back memories of how she had been at my age, when she was weighed down with kids that she hardly knew how to look after, and constantly bullied by the man who was supposed to be the love of her life. It's easy to see why she might want to shut out anything that reminded her of those times, and that perhaps made her feel guilty for the way in which she had abandoned her children. Whatever the reasons, I knew I was on my own with my problems.

The people at social services did their best to help me in every way they could, which meant we wouldn't starve and we had a roof over our heads, but I was desperate to do better than that for my precious child. I couldn't bear the thought that I could do no more than keep him alive. But what could I ever do to earn money? Dad had completely convinced me that I was no use to anyone and had ensured that I had no education or skills apart from street walking. The only thing I knew about was working on the Block, but returning to that option seemed too terrible to contemplate. I knew that I was lucky to have survived for as long as I had selling casual sex to strangers in cars. I dreaded the thought of being forced to go back to taking such enormous risks, but Dad had told me a million times that that was all I was good for, and in the increasingly frequent number of moments of self doubt I believed he was right.

Most children are lucky enough to have wise and kind guides to help them find their paths through life, mentors who have their best interests at heart and want to see them be happy and want to help them to thrive and succeed at whatever they choose to do. But what happens if the people you are forced to rely on for guidance at the very beginning of your life are not wise or kind? What if they are quite the opposite and do everything they can to tempt and force you down the wrong paths in life, being more interested in themselves and the gratification of their own desires?

No one can spend their whole lives blaming their parents for everything that goes wrong in their lives; after a while it comes down to the choices you make for yourself as an adult and you have to take responsibility for them, but how good or bad those choices are will very largely be determined by the foundations that have been laid in the early years of your life. I might have been eighteen years old when I had Brendan, but I still felt as completely lost as I had been at eight when I was forced to lie down beside Dad with those magazines and at thirteen when I sat in the cars of strangers and they did whatever they wanted to me.

One night when I was drowning in unpaid bills and utterly desperate for money, I left Brendan with a babysitter and went out onto the streets in search of motorists looking for business. The despair I felt as I climbed into those strangers' cars was the deepest and darkest I had ever experienced. I didn't ever want to go back to being that desperate. I only did it a couple of times but afterwards I sank into the blackest of depressions and decided I would rather end it all and let someone more responsible than me take over bringing up Brendan.

Since I was twelve or thirteen I had been cutting my arms with knives and any other sharp implement I could get my hands on. I just wanted to hurt myself because I thought I was so worthless I didn't deserve to be treated any better, to punish myself for being such a terrible person. I suppose it also gave me some kind of control over my body in ways that I didn't have otherwise. When the blood flowed, I always felt a sense of release, however momentary.

I started seriously trying to kill myself when I was about fourteen. The first time, I saved up paracetamol tablets by telling different people in the care home I was in that I had a headache or period pains and then swallowed them all one night but I was found and rushed to A & E to have my stomach pumped. I tried again not long afterwards but the same thing happened.

Whenever I was actually putting the tablets in my mouth I always intended to kill myself, but sometimes I would change my mind a few moments later. A kind of survival instinct cut in, making me panic and tell someone what I had done. They then raised the alarm and I was left with all the shame and embarrassment of having had my stomach pumped out and being given a load of lectures. With each failed attempt my self-esteem would shrink further.

Now, at the age of eighteen, I decided I had to make sure I died this time. I loved Brendan so much it hurt and I was terrified he was going to end up being damaged by whatever choices I made in life. Just looking at his perfect, innocent little face as I changed or fed him made me cry. But I had become increasingly certain I was the worst mother possible for him. He was helpless and trusted me completely but I believed that I had to let him go in order to give him a better chance in life than I had been given by my parents. I just wanted all the pain and shame to end and there only seemed to be one way to make that happen.

If I killed myself, Brendan would have a better life than I could ever give him and I would be released from my misery. I didn't think I deserved to live. I believed I was worthless, because that was what I had always been told by Dad and virtually everyone else I came across, and I now felt that I was so useless as a mother that even Brendan would be better off without me. On the evidence of what had happened so far, I didn't believe I was going to be capable of looking after him properly.

I didn't want to kill myself with him in the flat since I had no idea how long it would be before anyone found my body. My first priority was to ensure that he was somewhere safe before I did the terrible deed and ended the horrible charade of my short life forever.

I always tried to hide from everyone the fact that I wasn't coping but Doris, my social worker, had been able to see how much stress I was under beneath my seemingly cheerful, argumentative exterior. Doris had introduced me to a nice woman who worked as a foster mother and she had been doing a bit of babysitting for me, giving me a chance to get out and have a break now and then. As the darkness of my despair threatened to engulf me once and for all I took Brendan round to her house and asked if I could leave him with her for a while. She agreed immediately without asking any questions. She was a kind woman and I knew he would be in safe hands for as long as he was with her. I think perhaps I hoped that she would adopt him once I was gone, because she had already formed a bond with him.

It was agonising to say goodbye to the baby I loved more than anything in the world, to walk away from him feeling as if my insides were being physically torn from my body, but at the same time I was in a hurry now that I had made up my mind to get the whole thing over, eager to move on to a better place, or at least to be at peace, and to finally put an end to the pain. If Brendan was going to be better off being brought up by someone else I didn't want to have to be around to watch it happening; I wouldn't have been able to bear that. It was better that I acted quickly and decisively to end my life for everyone's sake. He would be free to get on with his life and I would be free of the pain.

I took him from his pram on the pretext of checking he was dry and comfortable, and held him for as long as I could bear, drinking in the scent of his skin as I kissed him for the last time and passed him across to the kind foster mother who had no idea of the turmoil churning around inside my mind. I was always good at hiding what I was feeling, giving people the impression that I was on top of everything, that I didn't have a care in the world.

After handing him into her care I left the house without looking back because I couldn't bear to see his trusting little face watching me go, and I walked straight back to my flat. I didn't want to think about anything else now that the final decision had been taken. It was a relief to be able to work on autopilot. The pain in my heart was so agonising I was frantic to numb it as quickly as possible.

I had been saving up paracetamol for weeks, knowing that this moment would come, that I would eventually have to admit defeat and give up Brendan and my life. Stockpiling tablets whenever the opportunity presented itself had been a habit of mine for many years. Knowing that I had them there was like knowing that there was an emergency exit available to me if life became intolerable. Having a potential way out sometimes made life seem a little more bearable during the years when I was with Dad or locked up in one children's home or another.

That morning, the moment I was alone behind my own front door I swallowed the tablets in greedy mouthfuls, washing them down with swigs of cheap wine. Then I sat down and waited for them to take effect, relieved to have finally made the decision to give up the struggle and to go on to somewhere peaceful. I was in a confused and emotional state already and once the tablets started working their way into my system reality became even more blurred, the world around me drifting into a sort of comfortable haze, a bit like a waking dream. The pain was fading just as I had hoped and life began to float away from me.

I could hear the phone ringing but I couldn't make any logical decision as to whether to answer it or not. In the end my hand just picked it up, like a robot, wanting to stop it from making such an irritating noise, and I put it to my ear. The deep voice on the other end was unfamiliar and I had to struggle to take in the words, forcing my brain to try to make sense of them and my mouth to respond in the way that the caller might expect. It sounded like a kind voice, someone who was trying to make a connection with me. It was probably only a few seconds but it seemed like an age before I realised it was a man called Rodney I had met a few days before, who had asked for my number. There must have been something comfortable and reassuring about him that had struck a chord because I had given him the number without hesitating, which I would never normally do with a stranger.

Who knows why he chose that moment to make a call? Maybe there was some higher force directing his actions, someone or something that wanted to stop me from doing what I was doing, or maybe it was just a lucky break.

I forced my brain to focus on what he was saying. It sounded as though he was asking me out. I didn't have the nerve to tell him I couldn't accept the invitation because I would be dead in a few hours' time. I don't know if the words that were coming out of my mouth were even making sense by that stage as I strained to make normal conversation.

The call from Rodney gave me a cause to hope, a tiny straw to cling to. It sounded to my desperate ears as if he was my knight in shining armour. When you are as near to the edge of the precipice as I was, the smallest thing can tip you either way. Just hearing from another human being, knowing that someone out there thought it was worth picking up a phone to call me, that this man was actually wanting to get to know me, made things feel different. By the time I finished the conversation and hung up, my life no longer seemed to be the same terrible black hole of despair it had been just a few minutes earlier. I had even managed to make a date to meet him, but meanwhile the drugs I had put into my system were well into the process of closing my life down.

Now that things weren't as painful and bleak as they had seemed before his call I no longer wanted to die but my head felt so heavy I wanted more than anything else to lie down and go to sleep. This stranger on the phone had thrown me a lifeline and I grabbed it, battling to stay awake, knowing that once I gave in to sleep that would be the end, that by the time anyone found me I would be long dead. I had to keep going, but the drugs had penetrated deep into my blood by then, relentlessly doing their work of shutting everything down. I had just enough brain cells functioning to know that I couldn't do this on my own, I had to get help.

I didn't have the strength left for more than one phone call by then. Not able to think of anyone else to turn to as I struggled to stay awake, I forced myself to concentrate for a few more seconds and dialled my mum's number. If my brain had been functioning logically I would have tried to think of someone else. This was the woman who had disappeared for most of my childhood and although we were back in contact again, there was no maternal bond between us. But in those moments, as my life was slipping away, I wanted my mum to be the one who was there for me. No way would I ever have wanted to rely on her for support or advice if I had had a choice – but I didn't. She was my only chance.

As soon as she answered I somehow managed to make her understand what I had done despite the fact that I could hardly get the words out. She made it clear to me that she was pissed off to have me messing up her day but a few minutes after hanging up the phone and lying back on the verge of surrendering to sleep, I heard the distant wail of an ambulance siren responding to her call. I was drifting in and out of consciousness by the time it arrived at my door and fell silent, replaced by the sounds of running feet and banging doors. At that moment I gave in to the tablets, knowing I was no longer alone as I slipped into unconsciousness, only vaguely aware of feeling myself being lifted onto a stretcher.

In hospital, after I had my stomach pumped, a psychiatrist came to talk to me, and then within a day they were releasing me back to my old life and all the problems that came with it. I was terrified that now they would take Brendan into care but to my surprise, Doris gave such a glowing report on my mothering skills that they didn't even mention it. They said they weren't surprised I felt suicidal after everything I had been through in my life and that they would look around for more ways to support me.

I'd been given another chance. Now it was up to me to try and make it work.

Chapter Three

A Ready-made Family

When Rodney first spotted me from the window of his van as I pushed Brendan's pram along the pavement, there was no way either of us could tell anything about the other. He must have seen an eighteen-year-old girl that he fancied and guessed from the fact that I was pushing a baby around that I was a mum, but he wouldn't have been able to even begin to imagine what the first eighteen years of my life had been like and that beneath the aggressive, cheeky exterior that I showed to the world there lurked a damaged little girl who lacked all self-esteem and any hope for being able to build herself a better future.

Likewise, I just saw a bloke in a van who had asked for my telephone number. I'd seen enough men through the windows of cars since I was twelve to know that they were seldom planning anything pleasant. He didn't look like anything special. I couldn't tell then if he was a knight in shining armour sent to save me from my past, or yet another useless man who was only after one thing and would either let me down or treat me badly. To be honest I wouldn't have given it that much consideration at the time, my thoughts being dominated by my own inner demons and my worries about how I was going to feed and look after my baby.

Rodney was a short, stockily built man, and not bad looking. You wouldn't say he was exactly handsome but he had a way about him that was attractive to people. My previous experiences of men hadn't only been with callous abusers like my father and the many punters and kerb-crawlers that he steered me towards over the years. There had been kind men too, like Brian, but in the end even the good ones turned out to be a bit hopeless at managing their lives, and were completely unable to offer me any of the guidance or support I needed as I stumbled to find a way to give my child a decent start in life. These men were as lost as I was, more so in most cases. Nearly every-one I knew had been led into using drink or drugs unwisely as they searched for ways to escape from the grim reality of their lives and themselves. Their addictions usually hastened the collapse of everything else in their lives, blighting their relationships, draining them of money and often making them unemployable. There was no way of telling if this man who had shouted out to me from his van was going to be any different or whether he would just add another level of pain to my life.

After I got out of hospital following the overdose I met Rodney for our first date in a pub in Norwich. He told me he came from a big gypsy family, who were all very close-knit, and that he came as part of a complete package, with a ready-made family of three children. There was Shiralee (more commonly known as 'Fred'), who was eight, Roddo, five, and Billy, who was two. To complete the family unit Fred also had a Jack Russell terrier called Midge, who had been with her since she was a baby and seldom if ever left her side. I told him about Brendan and about the fact that I had no contact with his father any more. We'd been chatting like this for a while when who should walk in but my Dad, now released from jail.

I introduced them and they got on like a house on fire, Rodney doing his best to make a good impression with the father of the girl he was interested in. It was only when we got back from the pub that night that I plucked up my courage and confided in Rodney about everything that Dad had done to me as a child, how he had raped me constantly and then started selling me when I was just thirteen. Even for someone as accepting and worldly as Rodney my childhood stories were a terrible shock. I told him about the first time Dad sold me, before he took me up to Ber Street, and how he had actually helped to hold me down.

'He had a friend called Peter,' I explained. 'A big, fat, smelly Irishman who was always working away from home and always had plenty of cash in his pockets when he came back.'

I could see that Rodney was becoming tense, as if trying to control his anger so as not to frighten me, forcing himself to listen to something that he knew was going to be horrific.

'They took me out drinking with them one night. At the end of the evening we went back to Peter's flat, picking up a Chinese on the way. It was a horrible, filthy place but I didn't care because I was happy to be with Dad. We were sitting on the settee, eating the Chinese when Peter started making a pass.'

I could still remember the whole night with horrible clarity, even though I had been very drunk. I remembered how I felt all excited to be treated like a grown-up when they took me out, like one of them. Peter's flat was a horrible, filthy place, where you'd expect to find winos living, but I didn't care because I was happy to be with Dad.

When Peter reached over to grab me I tried to get his hands off without making a fuss, thinking that Dad would punch him if he wasn't careful and wanting to avoid the evening turning into a brawl. The next thing I knew I was thrown on the floor amongst the scattered Chinese food cartons and Dad was pinning me down by the arms while his friend did what he wanted to me. I was struggling and shouting and Dad was telling me to 'shut up and relax' because it was going to happen either

40

way. I knew at that moment he had sold me and I remember staring at the overturned cartons on the carpet around me while it was going on and thinking that was all I was worth to my own father.

As I told Rodney the story I noticed that he was clenching and unclenching his fists, his lips tight and his eyes narrowed. Part of me was ashamed to let him know such terrible things about me, but the other part was relieved to have someone who cared and who was willing to listen.

'You mustn't see him any more, Ria. That man doesn't deserve the name "dad" after what he's done to you. I can't believe I was chatting away to him earlier. I'd have taken him outside if I'd known.'

He made me promise that I would stop seeing Dad and I was happy to agree. Even on our first date I realised that Rodney was different, that he was a man who seemed to know what he wanted from life and how he was going to get it, and I liked that. It felt like this might be the start of something important.

From the beginning Rodney was eager to start a relationship and it seemed to me as though he was the answer to all my dreams. I had always said I wanted to get married and have four children and now it looked as though my prayers had been answered in the most dramatic way.

Rodney immediately took charge of my life, moving into the flat with Brendan and me. I asked why we couldn't move to his but he explained that he lived in a caravan, and that there wouldn't be room for all of us. He was proud of his travellers' roots and was often disparaging of those of us who had been born and brought up in houses, calling us 'Gorjers'. But he seemed more keen to get into my flat, and any other house that I might be able to arrange for us as a family, than he was to live in a caravan or on the road. But that was all fine with me.

The next step was for me to meet his kids, and that all went perfectly. He saw them every weekend and during the school holidays, and so they would come round to stay in my flat at those times. Almost overnight I had gone from being suicidal, alone and frightened to being at the centre of a social whirlwind. Not only did I now have a man in my life, I also had four children, just as I had always imagined I would – plus a dog. Ever since I could remember I had wanted to be part of a proper family. I had no real idea what that would consist of; I just knew that I had never had one in the past.

At eighteen I probably seemed more like a friend or a big sister to Rodney's kids than a new mum, and all three of them accepted me immediately. I've heard lots of horror stories about the difficulties new wives have with their stepchildren, but I never had anything but friendliness and support from any of them. They also accepted Brendan as their new little brother without seeming to give the matter a moment's thought, happy to share their family with both of us. It was wonderful to watch Brendan's little face lighting up when they played with him and made him feel loved. They must have been so secure in the love of their dad and mum that they didn't feel remotely threatened or resentful about Brendan and me suddenly turning up in the middle of their lives.

My flat only had two bedrooms but we would all squash in somehow when the kids were there. Brendan had a cot and sometimes Billy would sleep in that and they would all swap and change around as the mood took them, usually ending up in the double bed, so that Rodney and I had to have the couch in the living room or a mattress on the floor. It didn't bother us; it was all about mucking in together as a family. I liked the times I had on my own with Brendan, but both of us always looked forward to the weekends and the other kids arriving, bringing a rush of excitement and distraction in through the door with them.

Brendan became just as keen to be around them as they were on him and he would cry inconsolably when Rodney dropped his new brothers and sister back to their mother at the end of each weekend because he would want to go with them. The others felt the same way, not liking it when they were separated.

The main reason why childhood had been such hell for me and my brothers was because both our parents always put their own feelings before everything else, never thinking of the effect their actions were having on us. Mum left Dad because she couldn't bear to have him forcing her onto the game all the time and, it seemed, without thinking what he would do to us once she was gone, and he used us as punch bags and ultimately turned me into a source of income in order to make his own life more comfortable. I was determined not to be like them. I wanted to always put my children first.

If there was one thing that made the idea of being with Rodney irresistible it was those children. With them around the house I could recreate the life that my brothers and I had never been allowed to enjoy because we had been split in half, with Terry and me staying with Dad and being kept apart from Chris and Glen once they were fostered out. We never had the chance to be one big noisy, chaotic, happy family. Even when we had all lived together in one house with Mum and Dad I had never had a chance to get to know Chris and Glen because they were locked upstairs in their bedroom.

My little council flat, which had seemed so deadly quiet and cold when it was just me and a sleeping Brendan, now buzzed with family life. I soon realised that Rodney was a brilliant father in many ways, totally supportive and 'there' for his kids. It was a startling contrast for me when I thought back to all the hours that Dad had spent inside pubs while Terry Junior and I either sat outside or waited at home, with no idea when we would see him again or what mood he would be in. Now that I was watching a good father at work it made me feel all the sadder for the things that I had missed out on.

Another great benefit to being with Rodney was that he had money, and he was generous with it. The ways in which he earned a living were probably similar to the ways his ancestors had been doing it for centuries. When I met him he was buying and selling cars and trucks without bothering much about official details such as registration papers. He always had a wallet full of cash in his pocket, although most of the time I had no idea where it had all come from, and as far as I could make out he never bothered with any paperwork. He had never learned to read or write, which was like my father, who didn't learn until he went to prison as a grown man. The difference was that whereas being illiterate embarrassed Dad, it didn't bother Rodney in the least. When we first met he said he'd teach me to drive and I could teach him to read and write in exchange, but although I did learn to drive he never got around to reading. He went to adult education lessons once to try to learn, but he didn't have the patience to persevere, especially as he was able to manage perfectly well without it.

It was an attractive, carefree attitude to life which appealed to someone of my age, much as I used to be impressed by Dad's swagger when I was a small child gazing with awe as he got a friend to drive him in a Jaguar to pick up his dole money, or he would ostentatiously light a cigar with a ten-pound note after a win on the horses. Rodney had the same lack of interest in convention or authority, but without my father's tendency to show off and boast about it. It was just the way he was. I would never know what car I would be driving from one week to the next. I could come home of an evening and find he'd sold the car I'd been planning to go shopping in.

'So?' he'd say when I complained, unable to see what the problem was. 'Take the truck.'

I actually enjoyed that side of his character, the unpredictability and the spontaneity. Once he'd bought a truck or a car he would immediately be stripping it down and changing the engine over, which was a skill he had taught himself over the years of dealing with scrap vehicles in places like his dad's yard. I guess he must have been tinkering with engines since he was tiny and understood instinctively how they worked. I once had to phone him from a petrol station where I'd stopped for fuel because I couldn't remember whether the van I was driving had a petrol or a diesel engine now.

Like his dad he was always working, always thinking, always doing deals, always looking for an angle. It was nice to have a man like that looking after me, having never been able to rely on my idle father for anything, never even knowing if there would be food on the table at the end of a day.

Money went out as easily through Rodney's hands as it came in, which sometimes made me nervous. And he was never one for paying the bills that I thought were important, like our rent or the poll tax. If I challenged him he would shrug and claim it was the 'traveller' in him, firmly keeping his wallet in his pocket and leaving me to find the money somewhere else if I was so keen to pay it. He might have thousands of pounds on him some days but if I asked him for some rent he would always say no. I didn't like that. Ever since having Brendan I had always wanted everything straight and above board, all my bills paid. After my childhood I didn't ever want to be dealing with bailiffs or debt collectors or social workers again if I could help it. I wanted things to be secure and legal. Since Brendan was born, I had this deep-seated fear of social services saying I was an unfit mother and coming to take him away from me and I didn't want to give them any excuses to do so.

Even with all this new family life buzzing around me Brendan was still the centre of my life and I was determined not to do anything to risk losing him or to mess up his chances in life. If I ever did get into debt it would worry me incredibly until I had managed to pay it off. I didn't want to give anyone a reason to think that I had failed in my attempt to be independent and to be a good mother. I had done enough failing in my life.

Most of all I wanted to prove to Dad that I could manage without him. Ever since I was a small child he had told me how useless I was and how I would never be able to manage without him. That had been how he had managed to force me to keep silent when he was abusing me himself, and how he could get me to go out to sell myself on the streets over and over again despite the fact that I hated it and was terrified every time. I never wanted to give him any chance to say that I had messed up my life once I'd left him so it made me nervous whenever Rodney took risks with my home and security. The worst thing would be to have to go back to Dad and ask for shelter, mainly because I didn't want to have him anywhere near Brendan. I had to keep Brendan safe and protected at all costs, which meant I had to do everything possible to keep a roof over my head.

Rodney might not have liked wasting his money on annoyances like rent and poll tax, but when it came to spending on life's pleasures he was never mean – far from it. After so many years of scrimping and scraping and having to sell my body or steal just to survive, it was like having a ten-ton weight lifted from my shoulders. For the first time in my life I was able to walk around a supermarket and just put whatever I wanted into the trolley, knowing that Rodney would happily pay the bill when we got to the till. For so many years I had felt like an outsider in this world, like some Victorian street urchin with my nose pressed up against a shop window, watching other people leading lives of what seemed to me to be unimaginable luxury but which was in fact just normal. Suddenly I could behave like all these normal people. It was a heady experience. I'd always been more used to buying one or two items at a time down the corner shop, existing from one makeshift meal to the next, always wondering if I had enough change in my pocket to manage till the next day. When you have been brought up in a house where there was never any money and where you only went into supermarkets in order to nick drink for your father, it felt like a dream come true; a shopping experience amongst the packed supermarket aisles that would be a chore for most people was like a day out in a theme park for me.

In one jump I had gone straight from being a suicidal teenage single mum, struggling to survive from day to day, to being a full-time stepmother and wife from the first day that Rodney moved into my life. In many ways, when I was busy and distracted, it felt like it was the most natural thing in the world, as if none of the pain and anger and resentment in my past had ever existed. Whenever Rodney was in charge there was always too much going on for me to have time for introspection and self-doubt, too much work to be done, too many people talking at once, too many surprises. There was no time to think about Dad or to remember the terrible times he had put me through, the memories that still haunted my nightmares. I thought that was a good thing. I thought that with Rodney's help I really was going to be able to put everything behind me and be happy. There were moments when I actually felt like I might be a worthwhile person after all.

* * *

One of the first things I had learned about the new man in my life was that he was from a big gypsy family. I guess I had a fair number of preconceived ideas about gypsies, probably most of them emanating from Dad, although God knows no one in our family was in any position to look down on anyone else. I had always been told they were dirty and dishonest and aggressive and so I have to admit I felt nervous at the prospect of meeting Rodney's extended family. I guess I never expected people to like me or love me because that had always been my experience. My own mother had left me, my father spent his whole time telling me how worthless and unlovable I was and his mother, my grandmother, never made any secret of how much she disliked having me around. I had no reason to think that Rodney's parents would be any more welcoming but I needn't have worried. They were great, accepting Brendan and me without a moment's hesitation.

As soon as Rodney and I became a couple, Brendan and I were considered part of their family. They never asked me any questions about where I came from or who my family were; they were totally accepting and non-judgemental. It felt as though I could start my life again with a clean slate. I didn't need to worry that they were talking about me behind my back or feeling sorry for me or disapproving of me because they were never like that. They weren't interested in anything that I might have done or that might have been done to me in the past, only in how I was now, just living in the present, dealing with the day-to-day business of making a living and looking after the baby. It was a wonderful feeling to be with people who weren't trying to bully or manipulate or humiliate me, who didn't want anything from me.

Rodney's parents lived in a caravan, which they had parked on a patch of land they owned out in the countryside, about eight miles outside Norwich. When Rodney first took me out there I was gob-smacked by how beautiful the location was. The caravan was immaculate, cleaner than any home I had ever been into, and full of bone china cups and sparkling cut-glass vases. In fact, it hardly looked lived in at all, more like a show home to be admired rather than actually used. The family spent most of their time in a shed that they had built on the site and which they had hooked up to a generator for electricity and heat. They used the shed as their office, their kitchen and a family meeting place. There were always a group of men sitting around talking about business and drinking tea, often with children running around at their feet.

I was amazed by how hygienic everything was as I watched Rodney's mum and the other women use different bowls for everything; the one designated for washing dishes was never used for anything else. I guess it comes from living on the road and not always having the luxury of permanent running water.

I had a look round Rodney's own caravan, which was parked on the site, but we never lived there, as my flat was a lot more comfortable. When I was feeling insecure (as I often was) I wondered whether my flat was as much of an attraction to him as I was, but in those early days and weeks I tried to push away my worries. My dreams had come true. I had a wonderful man, with a big family who accepted me as one of them, and four children to take care of. Relationships with new partners are always strange adventures. You set out hopefully, knowing nothing about the person you have just met, and gradually travel further and deeper into the complex jungles of emotions caused by whatever has happened in their pasts, and in yours.

Rodney's dad, Dick Drake, ran the main part of his business from the land around his caravan, stripping down old cars and trucks, repairing them if he could or dealing in the scrap metal that he was able to salvage. He was always working, always making a living wherever he could, always keeping his eye out for an opportunity to make a profitable deal. He owned another scrapyard further away from Norwich in Buxton, where I worked with Rodney all through our first winter together. Their plan was to clear the land because they were trying to get planning permission for houses so they could sell it on to a developer at a profit. There were hundreds of rusty old lorries and cars piled up there that needed to be dismantled, carted off and sold.

Despite the fact that it was hard work, especially on cold days, it seemed a romantic lifestyle to me, nothing like I had imagined it would be from all the things I had heard being said about gypsies in the pubs by people who didn't actually know any. Everyone who knew Dick loved him because he was the genuine article, a tiny, wiry little man, only weighing seven or eight stone, with a trilby hat permanently set at a jaunty angle on his head, always laughing, always friendly.

I soon learned that all the gypsy families stick together and are totally loyal to one another. I guess it happens with any people who have been as persecuted down the ages as they have. Having come from parents who could never be relied on for anything by anyone, not even to protect us or be there for us, it was a revelation. Such ferocious loyalty has its downside too, of course, and can often lead to disagreements breaking out when family members clash with the outside world and others wade in to support them, particularly when there is drink involved. There were a lot of fights going on, especially when we went out to the pubs. I had seen fights before when I was a child, and I had seen a lot of violence at home with Dad, but I had never seen anything like the level of violence the gypsies were capable of when they felt they were being threatened or disrespected. Even the women fought like men, never hesitating to get stuck into the thick of it, landing punches and doling out vigorous kickings to anyone who got in their way. I witnessed a lot of pubs being wrecked during those years as every stick of furniture was smashed up and turned into a weapon.

Rodney himself was never a man to go looking for trouble, but he was never one to back down if it came along either. If an argument was nothing to do with us he might walk away, but more often there would be a reason why he would be at the centre of it. I took my role as his partner very seriously and would stand by him in public whatever happened, even if it meant landing a few good punches myself. I had some experience of fighting because Dad would actually encourage Terry and me to fight when we were little, urging us on to punch each other properly and not just pull hair and scratch. I remember one time I made Terry's lip bleed with a punch and I felt terrible about it but Dad praised me and wouldn't let Terry hit me back.

There was never any telling when his violence would explode. I remember an argument with a lodger who had eaten Dad's chocolate biscuits by mistake. He beat the poor guy to a pulp in front of us, splattering the sitting room in his blood as he punched and kicked and threw him around, getting all his stuff and hurling it out into the street.

In some ways it was good to release some of the anger that I had pent up inside me after all the years when I had been unable to fight back against Dad because I was too little, too powerless. That's why I sometimes let myself be drawn in to fights, particularly when it was to defend another member of Rodney's family.

He was a real believer in families sticking together and although he continued to insist I had no contact with

Dad, he worked hard at trying to repair my relationship with Mum. She had broken up with her partner now, so she was able to come out with us without fear of angering him. If it was Mothers' Day or Christmas, Rodney would be the one telling me to ring Mum up and invite her out for dinner. It was as though he wanted to build a relationship with her to make up for the fact that he didn't get on that well with his own mother. I was happy for him to do that because I wanted to have her in my life and was pleased that she always agreed to whatever we suggested. I wanted my children to know their grandmother. After Mum left home I hadn't seen or heard from my maternal grandparents again for eight years. I remembered all too acutely what it felt like to have no relations who would send me a card on my birthday or a present at Christmas, and I was determined to do everything I could to give my children as big an extended family as possible.

My father's mother was the only grandparent who had been around in my childhood and she had never even pretended that she liked me. Dad had been the centre of her world and when I finally told the police about what he had done to me she never forgave me. When he was taken to court and convicted for living off my immoral earnings she was waiting outside to scream abuse at me as I came out in front of the whole world, calling me a whore and a liar. She knew everything about Dad and his lifestyle, so she knew that I was telling the truth, but she couldn't forgive me for sticking up for myself and for denouncing Dad in public. I suppose she thought I had betrayed her family in some way.

I wanted Brendan to have nicer memories of his grandmother than that. I could never understand why Mum's parents had wanted nothing more to do with us once Mum had left. Why had they not even sent us cards at Christmas or on our birthdays? Why had they acted as though we didn't exist? What could I possibly have done to offend them so terribly by the time I was six years old that they would want nothing more to do with me? Their disappearance had served to reinforce the idea in my head that Dad must be right, that I must be worthless and unlovable and that he was the only one who was ever going to care for me. I never wanted Brendan to think such thoughts about himself for even a second.

I have to admit that Mum could be good company on these family outings, if I could forget about all the resentment I had stored up inside me about what had happened in the past. When we were all together as a family and everything was buzzing it was often possible to ignore the little voices in the back of my head that were goading me on to ask her why she treated us the way she did. While part of me longed for us to all get on like one big happy family, another part always wanted to punish her in some way for her crimes against her children. The logical part of my brain would tell me that there was no point thinking like that. Rodney was right;

what was past was past and there was no point dwelling on it. But those voices were always there, even if I managed to drown them out with noise and distraction for most of the time.

I'm not saying Mum's life was easy, but then whose life is? Once I was a mother myself I couldn't understand how she could bear to let eight years drift by without even trying to do something to help her own children. When you have children of your own running around it focuses your mind on what happened to you when you were their age and makes you see things afresh. There was no way I would let Brendan anywhere near a monster like my father, not even with me there to protect him, so how could she have left us completely alone with him like that?

I didn't ask her, though. Not then, at least.

Chapter Four

Rodney and Me

Rodney was a brilliant family man. His commitment to his children was total and from the first moment we got together he included Brendan in that. Whenever the kids were with us he would be coming up with ideas for things to do with them, like driving off into the countryside, all of us piled into the cab of one of his trucks together, and having a picnic. Or we would go for a barbecue on the beach. He would always include Mum in these outings as well, arranging to pick up her and my young half-brother Adam who had been born in 1981, when I was fifteen.

Rodney might have been a bit stricter with discipline sometimes than I thought was absolutely necessary, but the kids all appeared to forgive him the odd smack and had grown used to being shouted at when they didn't obey him immediately. He insisted on instant obedience from all of us, but I was more than used to that. I had spent endless hours locked in the coal shed at home when I was small for some petty or imagined misdemeanour: sitting shivering in the dark, terrified by every sound but too frightened to call out to be released because it would result in a terrible beating, and desperate to win back Dad's approval. I knew all about the tyrannical ways in which some fathers chose to rule over their families. Although Rodney's kids were always respectful of him, and cautious about upsetting him, I could see they weren't actually frightened of him in the way Terry and I had been of our father. They could have a laugh and a joke with him in a way I could never have dreamed of with mine.

There are always people in any extended family or group of friends who are keen to stir up trouble for a newcomer to their social circle, as much for their own entertainment as anything I guess, and malicious voices were quick to tell me that Rodney's ex-wife Sue and I were bound to end up clashing. They told me, with mock concern for my welfare, that Rodney was still in love with her and that Sue was certain to resent me having anything to do with her children. I didn't like having this threat hanging over my head and I couldn't get a straight answer out of Rodney about any of it, so I decided to take matters into my own hands.

Plucking up all my courage I went round to her house to see her, wanting to set the record straight, to clear the air and make sure she didn't think she could take any liberties with me just because I was young. If there was one thing I had learned during my years of going in and out of care homes, it was that you had to stick up for yourself from the first moment you arrived in a new environment if you didn't want to end up being walked all over. In the past it had led to me getting a bit of a reputation for being hard in some of the institutions I had been in, when inside I had been no more than a scared, confused and insecure child.

The moment Sue opened her front door to me with a beaming smile on her beautiful face I knew we were going to get on. She invited me in as if it were the most natural thing in the world, as if she had been looking forward to getting to know me ever since she first heard I was on the scene. The moment I voiced my worries she assured me there was no way she would ever consider going back to Rodney, however much he might want it, and it was easy to believe her.

'To be honest,' she told me, 'I'm really glad that he's found someone else. Now perhaps he'll leave me alone and stop pestering me to go back to him.'

She introduced me to her new boyfriend, Kevin, who was only sixteen – a good few years younger than her. He was a gorgeous-looking lad and I could immediately see why she wouldn't be bothered about losing Rodney to me. At the time a lot of other people believed that Sue and Kevin's relationship couldn't last because of the age gap, but they were obviously totally in love.

The gossips and mischief-makers were just as wrong about Sue and me clashing because we never had so much as a cross word about the kids or anything else. From that day onwards we became best friends and got on so well that sometimes she and I would actually go together to the kids' parent/teacher meetings at the school. It made other people laugh to see us side by side but we didn't care and, more importantly, neither did the kids. I guess she must have been about the same age I was when she first met Rodney, so she understood very well a lot of how I felt and what I was going through as the years went on. Maybe she felt sorry for me because she knew what lay in store and because she had managed to escape to a relationship that was so much better.

During that first winter when Rodney and I were together, I went to work with him at the scrapyard. That was the way with all the wives in his family and I was always ready to do what he asked, even on the days when we were working in snow and ice and I thought my fingers were going to fall off every time I had to grip some freezing cold piece of metal and lug it onto a van. Rodney was a hard task-masker, expecting everyone else to work as hard as he did himself. He got the kids working for him too as soon as they were old enough and strong enough to lift things around. If he got home late from a job he would immediately send them out to load or unload the lorry for him. He would not tolerate any arguing or complaining. It was tough for them but it seemed acceptable because he worked so hard himself. It wasn't like Dad putting me to work on the streets and then disappearing into the nearest pub with his mates, only popping out occasionally to make sure that I was pulling in the punters and not hanging back in the shadows. Rodney managed to make it seem as though we were all working in the same family business, pulling together towards a common goal.

Sometimes during the week, when the other kids were at school or back with Sue, I would take Brendan with me when we went to work, and he and I would play together in the cab of the lorry while Rodney laboured outside. Rodney liked to have us around for company and to keep an eye on me. He always liked to be surrounded by friends or family wherever he was. Sometimes, when there was a lot for me to do at the job site, I would leave Brendan with a babysitter if I thought I wouldn't be able to keep an eye on him while I was working. Although I loved him to bits it was still nice to have the occasional respite from continuous baby talk.

In the summer months most of Rodney's jobs were to do with gardening, especially laying out patios and driveways; he was a skilful craftsman whenever he got the chance to show it, always doing a good job for his customers. My jobs would usually be to drive the van or mix the cement, or do any odd chore he asked of me.

Sometimes we would be clearing away scrap, like the old vehicles in Dick's yard, and my first job would be to get the wheels off. I grew strong from the physical labour of it and I liked how that felt. I felt as though he needed me, as though I had a role in his life, and it seemed like useful, honourable labour, not like the furtive, grubby work that Dad made me do with the men he made me sell my services to.

A couple of times a year Rodney and I would go to the horse market, held in the cattle market in Norwich, where all the old boys like Dick would be sitting around drinking and singing in the same way their ancestors must have been doing for centuries. It seemed very different to the sordid, claustrophobic little world of hookers, drunks and ne'er-do-wells that my dad used to live in. Dad liked nothing better than to be thought of as 'a bit of a character', always showing off and trying to attract a crowd in whatever pub he was in, but Dick didn't have to try that hard because everyone was auto-matically enchanted by him. After the sale had finished everyone would gather in the pub, The Norfolk Dumpling, and have a singalong and a good old drink. Quite often one of the little Shetland ponies would be brought into the pub to share in the fun. The children loved it.

Dick battled for years to get permission to build on the site of the Buxton scrapyard, even taking his case to the Court of Human Rights, claiming that he was being discriminated against because he was a gypsy. His perseverance paid off and he was eventually successful, but the deal didn't finally go through till after his death in 1989. Now they've built bungalows on the site and named it Drake's Loke in his honour. It was a shame he didn't live to see the fruits of his labours.

Dick's funeral was an amazing event, with travellers and relatives arriving in lorries from every corner of the country to pay their respects, partying long into the night to celebrate the life of a man who everyone seemed to have loved. No one could find a bad word to say about him, living or dead. According to the traditions of gypsy law, Dick's caravan should have been burned after he died but it never happened for some reason and Rodney's younger brother moved in and took over running the yard. Phoebe moved into a house in Buxton and Rodney and I got on with our own lives and our own family.

Anyone meeting me during those years would have assumed I was a full-blooded gypsy wife. I jangled with the gold jewellery and sovereign rings that Rodney would give me. I would be tanned from working in the outdoors and I hardly ever bothered to wear shoes when we were out and about, enjoying the freedom of bare feet, feeling like I was being a bit of a rebel. Rodney didn't allow me to do anything that might attract other men, like wearing make-up or skirts, but that didn't bother me too much as I had no sense of personal identity at that stage anyway. I only really existed as his woman and the kids' mother. I also liked the fact that it was very different to my days with Dad, when he used to make me get all dressed up in his prostitute friends' clothes and heels, and paint my face when I was as young as twelve. He would take me to parties like that to show me off, flirting with me as though I was his girlfriend, paying me compliments, pleased to see other men eyeing up the goods that he was soon going to be selling, or helping himself to as soon as we got home. Because Dad spent so much time telling me how fat, ugly and unlovable I was, I partly enjoyed it when he seemed pleased with the way I looked, but at the same time I already knew it was wrong and spooky for him to be paying me that sort of attention.

With Rodney it was completely the opposite and I liked that protectiveness to start with. I felt pleased that he loved me enough to be jealous of other men, instead of being happy to sell me to anyone with the price of a few drinks in their pocket, as Dad had been. Despite my low self-esteem I had always been good at putting on a brave face to the outside world and was always happy to chat to other people. Although I was pleased that Rodney was protecting me, I began to get confused when he was angry with me for talking to other men in normal social situations like pubs or shops. If I even put on a bit of lipstick when we went out together he would immediately accuse me of having an affair and would turn it into a big argument.

'I saw the way you were looking at him,' he would shout once he got me back home. 'You were leading him on, flirting with him.'

'I was just talking to him,' I would protest, completely unable to understand what was going wrong between us and why he didn't trust me.

As time went by it started to make me mad because I had never given him the slightest reason to think that I would ever be unfaithful to him. I hated people who messed around like that because I had seen how unhappy Mum and Dad had made each other. Although it was intimidating sometimes, his possessiveness did in a way make me feel secure, but this self-confidence that I was beginning to build was badly shaken one day when I discovered that Rodney had slept with the babysitter, Tina.

Tina and I were friends and used to take turns baby-sitting for one another. I first felt uneasy about her relation-ship with Rodney one evening when we went round to collect Brendan, and Rodney commented on some semi-naked photos of her that were stuck on her fridge door. They had quite an intimate giggle about them and a few days later Rodney picked a fight with me and stormed out, saying he was going to stay at his caravan.

Walking past Tina's house a bit later I spotted his truck outside, which was odd because I'd talked to her earlier and she'd told me she was going out for the evening.

I let myself into the house as I normally would when I was picking up Brendan, and there were Rodney and the children sitting round the table having a meal. The kids were all in a state of undress, having had a bath, so it was obvious they were planning on staying over. Rodney and Tina made no secret of the fact that they were having a fling and I felt doubly betrayed, by my man and by my friend.

This was exactly the sort of pain that I had been hoping Rodney would protect me from and it brought back a million memories of my time with Dad, reminding me of all the reasons why I hated the way he and his friends behaved so casually about sex. We had an incredible row and from then on I kept Brendan with me nearly all the time rather than hiring another babysitter and putting temptation in Rodney's way. There was never any question that I would take him back – I needed him too much – but once someone has betrayed you, however, you can never feel quite the same about them again. Trust in a relationship, I believe, has to be an absolute; you either have it or you don't; there are no degrees in between.

In my heart I knew he had been unfaithful to me at other times too and I realised that since I didn't have the courage to leave him I'd have to put up with it and try to ignore it. He didn't even seem terribly concerned about hiding it from me after that. Perhaps he felt it was his right as a man. It certainly wasn't a subject he was prepared to discuss with me. All the confidence that had been building inside me, when I thought I had found a knight in shining armour to protect me, was draining away, leaving me feeling vulnerable and worthless all over again.

Despite whatever he might be up to himself when the opportunity arose, Rodney wanted to have me somewhere where he could keep an eye on me every hour of every day, and he would become more and more possessive if he thought I was even passing the time of day with any other men. Although I was still mistaking his behaviour for a kind of love it was making life difficult, making me feel stifled and restricted, as though I had no more freedom than I'd had when I was in Dad's power.

One day I had been out shopping for hours and when I came back I discovered that my period had started and I'd forgotten to buy any tampons. Rodney was home by then, outside in the garden with a couple of mates.

'I'm just nipping up the shop,' I told him as I headed back to the car, not wanting to go into any more detail in front of the other men.

'No, you're not,' he replied. 'You've been out all day.'

'You can't tell me I can't go up the shop,' I said. 'I need to go.'

'You're seeing somebody,' he shouted. 'You're not going out again. What could you need when you've already been out shopping all day?'

'I need some fucking Tampax,' I screamed at the top of my voice, no longer caring about being discreet, wanting to embarrass him in front of his mates to make him realise he was being stupid.

But he still wasn't having it and told one of his mates to go down the shop and buy them for me, which made the whole thing even more embarrassing for all of us.

'Get back in that house!' he ordered me.

There were days when I didn't feel like going to work with Rodney, just wanting to stay at home and look after Brendan rather than sitting around in the cab of the van in some unknown part of town, but he was always adamant.

'You're not staying here on your own,' he said. 'What are you planning to do anyway?'

'I could take Brendan out in the pushchair for a walk,' I said, fed up with being bossed about all the time, needing some space away from Rodney and his mates. 'It'll be nice for him to get some fresh air.'

'No, you're bloody not! I'm taking the pushchair with me,' Rodney said, snatching it up before I could get to it. 'So if you don't come with me you'll be staying in all day.'

That made me cross. I might have liked Rodney's possessiveness at the beginning, but this was stupid and felt more like bullying than love, more the way I remembered Dad behaving, bringing a thousand ugly memories to the surface. I started to shout back at him, genuinely angry, not for a moment expecting what was to come next. Rodney was used to total obedience from all of us.

He was only willing to put up with my back-chat for so long before his temper snapped. I pushed it too far this time and suddenly he punched me in the face with all his strength in order to put a definite end to the conversation. I didn't see the blow coming and for a moment I was too shocked to even register the pain as I hurtled backwards off my feet.

In that split second everything changed and I became a victim once more. Everything good that he had done for me was shattered with that one blow. There was nowhere I could be safe, not even my home, and no one I could feel safe with. I lay there feeling betrayed and destroyed, cowering in case he tried to hit me again, too shocked to respond in any way.

Leaving me lying there he stormed out of the flat to work, carrying the pushchair with him, no doubt feeling that he had succeeded in making his point.

I don't know why I was so shocked because I had yet to meet a man who didn't end up wanting to hit me, but I remember feeling suddenly trapped and scared as I lay there waiting for the pain to subside and trying to clear my thoughts. All the things that had become good about my life were due to Rodney being there, but this punch immediately made them worthless. The moment I knew that he was capable of hitting me so violently, using all his strength, I should have walked away from the relationship, but if I did that I would have lost the whole family that I had just found. I would have taken Brendan with me, but I wouldn't have had any claim on Fred, Roddo and Billy. I would have been deserting them just as surely as Mum had deserted us.

There was also a part of me that believed I deserved to be hit. All my life Dad had been telling me how worthless and unlovable I was and how he would be the only one who would ever love me and a large part of me believed him. The way I had been treated by the dozens of clients I had serviced for him on the streets of Norwich had reinforced everything he ever told me about myself. From the first time that Dad sold me to that mate of his, holding me down to be raped on the floor amidst the scattered remains of a cheap Chinese takeaway, I had believed that I didn't deserve anything better. If I was so worthless my own father was willing to do that, why should I be surprised that Rodney would hit me when I was giving him so much grief?

I pulled myself up onto a chair, still trying to clear my head and work out what I should do. My face was throbbing with pain, but what I felt inside was worse. It felt as if I was letting a piece of myself go, surrendering to the life that I could now see inevitably lay ahead of me. Until that moment I had felt safe with Rodney, but now I was frightened of him. The possessiveness that I had been quite enjoying, which had been making me feel cared for, now seemed threatening.

I should have packed and been gone before he got home from work, but I wasn't ready to do that. I didn't want to throw away everything we had together, but I became more wary after that punch, trying to work out what I should do. The arguments went round and round in my head. I knew that if I did leave, Brendan would be separated from the man he thought of as his dad, just as I would be separated from the other children, who I already adored as if they were my own. I was trapped.

At the same time, I started to think more carefully about the things that other people in the family were saying, asking more questions, and it suddenly became clear to me that Rodney was still in love with Sue, that he would have dumped me in an instant if she had agreed to take him back. I was sure I believed Sue when she said she was no longer remotely interested in Rodney and was perfectly happy with Kevin, but I still knew that if Rodney was in love with her then he couldn't be in love with me, however possessive of me he might be. What on earth was I doing with him?

I felt as though I was being torn in half, one part wanting to run away from the pain as fast as possible, the other terrified of making the same mistake as Mum by putting my own needs ahead of Brendan's. Both options filled me with horror and so I did nothing, trying to work out a way of living with the idea of being trapped with a man who didn't love me and was capable of violence towards me. I genuinely couldn't think what else to do.

Chapter Five

Husband and Brothers

It wasn't long before the council realised that we needed more space and allocated me a three-bedroom house, which we set about turning into a home. The house felt much more like a family home than the flat ever had, even though it was in a pretty bad state, having been neglected by previous tenants. Putting it right would have been too daunting a project for me on my own, but with Rodney it became an adventure and he was happy to let me stay at home to do some of the work on my own because it meant he knew where I was. At the same time I no longer minded being stuck in the house on my own if he was out because now I had a project to focus on. I was creating a nest for all of us and I threw myself into the task wholeheartedly. While he was at work I would be papering walls and painting doors and ceilings, amazing myself at what I was actually capable of achieving when I set my mind to it. The transformation as it progressed from room to room was the most satisfying thing I had ever done. It felt as though I had some control over my own surroundings for the first time in my life. I could actually make a difference to my surroundings, and to the children's.

Dad used to be good at DIY, but he only ever bothered to do it in the rooms that would be seen by his friends. In our bedrooms it was all ancient peeling wallpaper and bare boards. I found that I got even more pleasure from doing up the kids' bedrooms than I did from the lounge.

By keeping busy I tried to convince myself that all the good stuff that was happening in my life more than compensated for the fact that I was constantly frightened of angering Rodney in case he hit me again. I told myself that no one can have everything, but with every step forward I took with my self-confidence I was aware that the potential for violence from Rodney lurked out of sight in the background, threatening to explode at unexpected moments and drag me back down into a deep well of bad memories and fear.

It wasn't that I let him get away with whatever he wanted. I would argue back, threatening to leave. He didn't always resort to using his fists but he was always willing to do anything that would help him get his own way. The first time I carried through my threat and stormed out of the house with Brendan, Rodney tracked me down to a nearby friend's house and snatched Brendan away from me, leaving me no choice but to follow them home. I suppose I could have gone to the police and asked them to intervene but I might have had to wait for a court order to get Brendan returned and he was too little to be away from his mum for even one night.

I was more terrified of losing my son than I was of being hit. I always hated being parted from him for even a few hours, let alone a few days. It reminded me yet again of how Mum had left us (although I didn't have the same fears about Rodney's abilities as a father as she had about Dad's). I hated the fact that the kids sometimes got to see the violence and the rows between us, and I always felt very ashamed when they did, but I knew Rodney would never hurt them, beyond the odd bit of disciplining. He had proved over and over again that he was a good father, but in a way that made it all the harder for me to escape. If he had been a total monster like Dad I would have grabbed Brendan and run for my life until I was far enough away for him never to find me. My biggest problem was that even if I did decide to leave, I had nowhere else to go.

No one else in Rodney's family seemed to find anything wrong in his violent behaviour. I began to notice that a lot of the gypsy women sported black eyes and split lips on a regular basis and none of them ever mentioned how they came by them. It seemed as though it was normal for men to hit women; so normal it didn't even provoke a comment. I blamed myself for making Rodney angry so often, although I hardly ever knew what I had actually done wrong to inflame his anger. Sometimes I would be doing something as innocent as cleaning out the kitchen cupboards and he would come storming in and punch me on the nose, making the blood spurt everywhere. He wouldn't worry about whether the kids were there to witness it or not. I suppose it helped him to keep them in line as well if they knew what lay in store for them should they displease him.

Despite all this there were still more good times than bad. One day, for instance, Rodney dropped the kids off with me before jumping straight back into his car again.

'I'm going to fetch Roddo's Shetland pony, Tom Thumb,' he told me.

'How are you going to do that?' I asked, knowing that at the time he had no van, just the Chevrolet hatchback that he was zooming off in – but he was already gone.

An hour later I heard him returning and went back outside just as he drew up in the car. Climbing out he opened the back door as casually as if he was letting Midge the dog out and Tom Thumb, the pony, stepped daintily onto the pavement, immediately putting his head down to munch on the front lawn. Moments of laughter like that made me forget the bad times and feel glad that I had decided to stay with Rodney. Life was never dull.

Dick and Phoebe had a pony and cart, which we would sometimes borrow in order to take a whole mob of friends down to the pub on a Sunday afternoon, including a lot of overexcited children. On days like that I was aware of how good it felt to be part of a family and to be able to share such lovely experiences. I knew I had Rodney to thank for all the good times and that made me feel guilty for not being able to make him love me. At the same time, I realised I didn't actually love him either. I'd wanted to love him because I was desperate for the whole package that came with him, but I never felt a longing for him the way I knew some other women felt for their men.

After we had been in the house for almost a year we decided to move closer to Sue and Kevin so that we would be nearer to the children and Brendan would be able to attend the same school as them. Sue was as keen on the idea as we were and although I still suspected Rodney of wanting to get back with her, I knew for a fact she wouldn't have him back, so I agreed. For me, it would be wonderful to have such a good friend nearby. We moved into a house around 500 metres from them and after that, we no longer had to wait for weekends or holidays to see the kids. They could come and go as they pleased, which was wonderful for all of us.

At this time we had managed to acquire quite an array of animals. We had dogs, and a miniature goat, which we had to pass on because the neighbours complained about the noise. We had a big white duck called Doris, Roddo's pony Tom Thumb, and another Shetland pony that we had bought from the market, along with her foal called Arthur. There was an area of common ground close to the house and we would take the new pony and her foal over there every morning and leave them to graze for the day, collecting them later in the evening and leading them back home. All the children on the council estate thought it was magical, as many of them had never seen ponies before. If they asked we would give them little rides around the field.

Rodney and I were working together on the markets at that time selling clothes and one day we were tracked down by the police, who gave us the horrific news that the mother pony had been viciously attacked and killed with an axe blow to the head. It was devastating and the children were heartbroken. The front page of the local paper covered the story and the local people were almost as upset as we were. Everyone was talking about who the culprit might be. It wasn't long before we worked out what had happened. A week or so earlier, Fred had come back from the park where the kids used to play saying that a lad had asked Billy, who was five at the time, to do something sexual to him. We had all been really upset about it and a few days later the lad was beaten up for it, probably by some of the gypsy men. It turned out that his older brother, who worked in an abattoir, had decided to take his revenge. Used to slaughtering pigs, he knew just how to go about it and felled the pony with a single axe blow.

We told the police about this boy and that we'd heard he had been boasting about what he had done around the estate. I think they did question him before deciding there wasn't enough evidence to go on. A little while later I heard that the boy from the slaughterhouse had been beaten up quite badly. I never knew who had administered this retribution; sometimes there were things that I didn't want or need to know. A lot of people were appalled by the attack on our pony so I imagine it was someone in the gypsy community who had sought revenge on our behalf. We got a lot of letters of sympathy and some people even sent money to buy a replacement pony. People in the area were always very supportive of us, partly because we were involved in the local community centre for a while, running the bar and serving on the committee as well as being members.

Rodney had taken to making home-brewed beer around this time and we would have crates of Corona bottles in the cupboard under the stairs that would sometimes explode because he had put too much sugar in them. One evening he decided to make some elderberry wine and it seemed that every utensil in my kitchen was stained purple with the berry juice. Some traveller friends of ours had come round for a tasting and we started drinking in the garden on a sunny summer day. They had a gold necklace that we wanted to buy but they also wanted to buy the demijohn of elderberry wine. As we all became more and more tipsy, the price of the necklace and wine came down, but so did the amount of wine left in the demijohn. As bottles of homemade brew exploded like fireworks and we all became more drunk, I eventually got my gold necklace. On nights like that it seemed like a good life.

Rodney had started asking me to marry him pretty soon after we met and I genuinely didn't know whether to say yes or no. I spent many nights lying awake, my thoughts churning over and over and reaching no conclusions. We both wanted to have another baby because although we already had a big family we hadn't actually produced a child together. Maybe I thought that having his baby would bring us closer and make me feel differently about him. I was feeling especially broody because one of my friends had recently had a little girl and just holding her in my arms brought back so many wonderful memories of how it had felt to hold Brendan when he first arrived.

We wanted our baby to be as close in age to the others as possible and I also wanted us to make it official so that we would all have the same name. At that stage I was still using my family name, which I hated because so many people in Norwich knew all about Dad and our family. Brendan had his father Brian's surname and the other kids were all Drakes. I wanted the whole world to know that the Drakes were one big happy family. Getting married seemed the obvious thing to do to tidy up all the loose ends in one go, then we could change Brendan's name too since he never saw his birth father Brian, but at the same time I had the deepest misgivings about tying myself forever to a man who was capable of hitting me.

I was afraid Rodney wanted to marry me because he thought that would give him greater control over my life. Being a husband must be a comfortable position for someone who is a bit of a control freak.

At one moment, when my doubts became so heavy I felt I had to share them with someone, I even asked Mum what she thought I should do.

'If you don't love him,' she said, surprising me with her wisdom, 'you shouldn't go through with it.'

It was good advice. Although having said that, she and Dad had been so totally in love that they had messed up everything else in their lives, so maybe it is better not to marry someone if you are in the grips of some sort of mutual obsession. I wavered back and forth, trying to weigh up my personal reservations against the interests of all the kids. Any young woman would be nervous about committing herself to marriage, I reasoned, but things would probably work out okay. I might not love Rodney in the right way but I did respect him and need him, and I couldn't bear the thought of losing the beautiful family unit we had created together. I also thought that he might become less possessive if he felt we were safely married.

Thinking about becoming a permanent part of Rodney's family also made me think a lot about my own family and the way in which it had been allowed to disintegrate just because Mum and Dad couldn't live together. Although I didn't want anything at all to do with Dad, I found myself longing to put the rest of us back together again, to be reunited with Chris and Glen, my two little brothers who had been taken into care as soon as Mum left and who my older brother Terry and I hadn't spoken to again since that day, when I was six and they were only aged two and three.

There had been one occasion when they were brought back to visit our next-door neighbours soon after we were separated and Terry and I had seen them being taken in and out of the front door next to ours, but we had been told we weren't allowed to talk to them – God knows why the social workers thought it would be more upsetting for us to talk to them than to stand silently by, watching them through a window. I didn't even know where they were after that, or how I could go about finding them. All I knew was that they had been taken together to the same foster family and that things had been okay for them after that. The first few years of their lives might have been a nightmare of neglect and cruelty, but once they escaped from our house they'd had a better time than Terry and I had had, being left behind to fend for ourselves amidst the shambles of Dad's life.

Without consulting Rodney, I decided to do something positive about finding Chris and Glen and I contacted social services to see if they could help me get in touch. At that time Terry was still hanging around with Dad a lot and so I wasn't seeing much of him either because I didn't want to have any involvement with our father and because Rodney forbade me from seeing him anyway. I had successfully cut him right out of my life and I didn't want to give him any excuse to renew contact. There was still no way I wanted him coming anywhere near Brendan, and I didn't want him undermining me and telling me what a failure I was and how I should go back on the game. Terry seemed to be able to deal with Dad better now that he was an adult man and too big to get beaten up by him – or maybe he just couldn't find an alternative place to live.

Social services made some enquiries and came back with the news that both Chris and Glen had now left their foster home and were finding their feet in the outside world just like me. Glen, who was the youngest, was living in a bedsit in a halfway house designed to encourage independent living while still providing a bit of support, and Chris was living with friends. They had both said that they would like to be put back in touch with me.

I was so excited I couldn't even wait another day and immediately hurried round to see them. I went to find Glen first and my heart was thumping in my ears as I approached the address that I had been given. I had no idea what to expect. Would it be embarrassing? Would we have anything in common at all? Would we like each other? I didn't remember either of them from when they were kids but I needn't have worried because the moment Glen opened the door to me I knew it was going to be all right between us. He seemed as excited to meet me as I was to meet him. We bonded immediately.

I couldn't stop staring at him as we talked, searching for genetic clues. It was easy to see that he was my brother; we had the same colouring and freckles, like Dad. When I went on to meet Chris I found that he was dark, more like Mum and Terry. It felt so strange to see bits of myself in two grown men who were virtually strangers to me and about whom I knew almost nothing.

Glen was so easygoing and relaxed it would have been impossible to dislike him. He was a gentle giant of a guy and I felt proud to think he was my brother. He was epileptic so he was a little uncertain of himself and what was likely to happen to him next, not sure what he was going to be able to do or whether he was ever going to be able to lead a completely independent life. He couldn't learn to drive and he had already discovered that there weren't many jobs he could do, which meant he had a lot of time on his hands.

Chris was having less difficulty with life, although both of them were finding it hard to make the sudden transition from being part of a foster family to being expected to fend for themselves. The system often seems to let kids down at this stage. It's as if the authorities believe that the moment someone passes their sixteenth birthday they somehow transform from being a dependent child into a fully functioning adult. Anyone who has brought up children knows that nothing is that simple and that we all go on needing advice and support from our families for a lot longer than that. I can still remember clearly how helpless and lost I felt when I was seventeen and eighteen and living on my own before meeting Rodney, struggling to manage on virtually no money and trying to learn all the skills of being a grown-up overnight, with nobody there to advise or pick up the pieces when I made a mistake. It is a difficult period of life for anyone, even someone with every advantage and a strong family network behind them.

It was a lovely reunion with my baby brothers, just as I had dreamed it would be. It felt like a first step in mending a great many broken bridges and I resolved to become a part of their lives now and help them however I could.

By the time I got home that evening I was buzzing with excitement at having been reunited with such an important part of my lost past. I suppose I should have guessed that Rodney wouldn't share my enthusiasm but I was too full of my own excitement to give it any thought. When he found that I had gone out and done something without his knowledge or permission he was furious. When he then discovered that I had been to see my brothers he was even angrier. I knew how he felt about Dad and Terry, but I had somehow thought that he would understand about Chris and Glen, being as family-oriented as he was, but I very quickly realised my mistake. I suppose it was to do with his need to see himself as the one and only man in control of everything in his life, including me, and he didn't want me to have anything to do with anyone from my previous life who he couldn't control and keep an eye on, as he did with Mum. Perhaps he suspected my brothers wouldn't take kindly to him hitting me as often as he did.

Having been on such a high after meeting Chris and Glen, I felt deeply hurt that Rodney wouldn't support me in getting to know them, despite knowing how much it meant to me. Because he had such a huge extended family himself, I suppose he couldn't imagine for a moment what it felt like to have no one from your past who you could really love and trust. Mum might have been back in my life but after what she had done to us as children I was never going to be able to have a normal, trusting relationship with her. There were so many things I couldn't talk to her about without becoming angry, so many no-go areas for both of us, but with my brothers I had a real chance of starting our relationships afresh. I wanted to reclaim at least some of my family.

Over the following months I stayed in touch with Chris and Glen as much as I could, but meanwhile Rodney did everything he could to make the meetings uncomfortable and to make the boys feel so unwelcome in our house that I couldn't really involve them in the family in the way I would have liked. It was becoming clearer to me all the time that Rodney didn't want me to have any friends other than his.

Despite his objections, I still wanted to mend bridges and salvage as much as I could from the wreckage of my childhood, so one evening I arranged for Chris and Glen to meet Mum and me in a pub and, in the spirit of the family reunion, I invited Terry along as well. It was obviously a really difficult occasion for Mum and I could see she was very nervous when she arrived. It must have taken some courage. I suppose she wondered if we were all going to gang up and give her a hard time, but none of us wanted to do that. It was much too late to put anything in the past right, but we all thought there was a chance we might be able to start afresh and build a better family network for the future as long as Dad wasn't involved. It never occurred to any of us to arrange a reunion with him, knowing that he would take it over and then use it to give us all a hard time.

The boys were so friendly and eager to put Mum at her ease that the whole evening turned out to be really nice. Chris even went to live with Mum for a while after that as he tried to sort his life out, although it didn't work out in the long term. I never asked either of the boys how they felt about her. We all made a big effort to get on, but I have always believed I could feel an underlying current of resentment in them for the fact that she left us and that she never made any effort to rebuild her relationships with any of us. It was always up to us to invite her over or to ring her up. She never thought to make the first move, which I believe most mothers would do. In fact, now that I'm a mother myself I don't know how she stops herself from phoning her children all the time because I know that's what I want to do. It was always the same. Even on my half-brother Adam's birthdays she would never think to invite the rest of us over for so much as a cup of tea. It was almost as if she didn't know how to be a mother.

Maybe Chris and Glen didn't feel as strongly as I did because they were so much younger when she left and because they had good foster parents who filled some of the gaps that our parents left in our lives. Whenever I did try to talk to Mum about the past she seemed to swing back and forth, one moment claiming that she was feel-ing desperately guilty for what she had done and the next moment going into complete denial and blaming Dad for everything that had ever gone wrong in the family, in the same way as he used to blame her for ruining everything by breaking his heart and deserting us. Both of them have always been so busy thinking about themselves and their own great tragic love affair, or lack of one, that neither of them have ever given a thought to the effect their actions had on their children.

In 1987, at the age of twenty, I finally decided to ignore Mum's advice and my own qualms and go ahead and marry Rodney. Even though in my heart I wasn't at all sure that I was doing the right thing I couldn't put him off any longer. We changed Brendan's name to be a

Drake like the rest of us so we would all be one big family. We held the ceremony at the local registry office on a weekday afternoon and the only people who attended were my three brothers, Mum, her mum, the children, a couple of close friends to act as witnesses, and my former probation officer (I'd become really friendly with her after I got a couple of convictions for shoplifting during the time when I was trying to bring up Brendan on my own). Rodney didn't bother to invite any of his friends. I spent £20 on a new dress but we didn't have a reception, so I doubt if the whole afternoon cost us more than £100 – hardly the sort of wedding that every girl dreams of.

All through the ceremony I was feeling uneasy, but my worst moment of panic was just before I took my vows, when I experienced a horrible premonition that I was about to make the most terrible mistake of my adult life. I had an overwhelming urge to run away before it was too late. I glanced across at the children and they all looked so happy, watching us intently as we committed ourselves to staying together forever, that I didn't have the nerve to speak up. The only comfort I could find, as I tried to quieten the sickening feeling of dread in the pit of my stomach, was that if it did all prove to be a ghastly mistake I could always get a divorce; not exactly the most promising attitude with which to start a new marriage.

Chapter Six

Sticks and Stones – and Words Will Always Hurt Me

To a greater or lesser extent all the men I had ever met had seen sex as their right, believing they could do whatever they wanted and the woman just had to put up with it. Customers believed it because they had paid money for a service, Rodney believed it because he was my partner, and Dad had believed it because he always believed he could do whatever he wanted with any woman. Other boyfriends hadn't been much different. In fact the first time Dad penetrated me, as well as the time he had held me down for a client, he had advised me to 'stop struggling because it was going to happen anyway and I was only making it worse for myself'. As far as I was concerned that pretty much summed the whole thing up from then on.

Although I like to believe my father was an exception to the rule, even now I still fear that there is a little bit of that primeval attitude towards women left in a lot of men, certainly the ones I had met by that stage.

Rodney would expect sex every other night (generously agreeing to let me sleep on the nights in between), and once he'd had his satisfaction he would immediately turn over and start snoring. I would creep to the bathroom and scrub myself raw, just as I used to do when I was a teenager in care, trying to rid myself of every last trace of his smell from my skin. I would then curl up in a chair and weep in private, racking my brain for ways that I could escape from being Rodney's wife without losing all the good things about being part of the family.

I didn't hate Rodney for wanting and taking sex because I thought that the problem lay with me rather than him, but it was still bad enough to make me want to leave him every time it happened. I would tell myself that I was his wife and it was something I just had to do but I still felt violated and used, just as I had done with Dad. I used to read articles in magazines in which women talked about how they never had orgasms and never enjoyed sex, which made me feel less alone but led me to assume that I was always going to be like that too.

I guessed that it was because of what had happened to me as a child but it was something I really didn't want to think about at all if I could help it. I did manage to talk to Rodney about it once but we both assumed there was something wrong with me, it was the way things would always be, and that there was nothing we could do about it. There certainly didn't seem to be any way he would ever give up what he saw as his conjugal rights. I had no reason to assume that it wasn't the same for many other women, but the thought of having to go on putting up with so much unhappiness for years and years, until I was no longer attractive enough for men to want to bother with me, made me feel suicidal.

Despite all these problems, in many ways my first few years with Rodney were some of the happiest of my life, certainly happier than anything that had come before. However, I can see now, with the benefit of hindsight, that beneath the bustle and busyness I was in many ways still as miserable as I had been as a child when I was being forced to sell my body to strangers. It was as though I was leading a false life. Being Rodney's wife gave me an identity and I could keep myself distracted on the surface for most of the time, but inside I felt as though I was dead.

From the moment Rodney and I were married, I think he stopped wanting to get back with Sue. Everything changed for him; from then on he never wanted to lose me, just as he had never wanted to lose Sue up till that point. I suppose in a way I became a possession on the day I became his wife and that he now felt he had a right to own me forever. He actually became more possessive rather than less and it could be deeply scary sometimes.

I think he probably behaved exactly the same way towards Sue when he was married to her. We still got on like a house on fire and she never showed the slightest bit of resentment towards me because of my relationship with her children as they grew older. She was as happy as I was for them to wander back and forth between our two houses, deciding on the spur of the moment each day where they would eat or where they would sleep that night. She would often babysit Brendan for us and in many ways it was as if we were both sharing the workload of bringing up all the children. So often when friends have divorced I have seen how they almost tear the children apart with their insecurities, jealousies and resentments. It is such a shame because when sharing the children in an extended family works well it can produce the best and most secure family feeling imaginable. Sue and Kevin would often come round to join us for barbecues and family parties, just like Mum.

But if that side of things was working, another wasn't. From the moment we were married, Rodney's possessiveness seemed to grow worse. It was as if he felt he now had the right to treat me any way he wanted, and make me do whatever he wanted whenever he wanted. But I was growing bolder with age too, more willing to stand up for myself. Our arguments grew fiercer and more frequent and finally we had one fight that lasted for four whole days. I can't even remember what it was about in the first instance but it exploded into a huge explosive slanging match. It was the worst fight we had ever had and it seemed as though it could never end because neither of us was willing to give in. We had only been married for three months. Knowing that I would probably walk out on him the moment I had an opportunity, Rodney became paranoid as the fight dragged on and wouldn't let me out of the house, determined to keep me in his sight and under his thumb. Increasingly desperate when I refused to obey him totally he eventually ran out of rational arguments and patience and resorted to using his fists again in order to try to pummel me into submission.

'You just want to go running back to your father,' he shouted as he punched me over and over again, 'so he can rape you some more and put you back on the game!'

His terrible words were a thousand times more painful than the physical blows. They struck so deep into my soul that I can still feel their impact even today, over twenty years later. This man was my husband. He was supposed to love me and to protect me, yet he was willing to say something so hurtful and so unfair. I knew he hated it when I cried, just as Dad always had, but I couldn't stop the tears from coming as the words dug deep into my heart, making me feel unclean and making me realise that I was fooling myself if I thought I would ever be free from my father and my past. He saw my tears and laughed to realise that he had scored such a bull's eye, but when I couldn't stop myself from sobbing he became irritated and roared at me even louder.

'Stop crying!'

Frightened he was going to start beating me again I somehow managed to stem the sobs and swallow back the tears. It was as though I had dropped an iron barrier between my brain and my heart and I vowed to myself that I would never cry in front of him again. I knew at that moment that he had finally made it impossible for me to ever be able to love him. I think he must have shocked himself by saying those things that day, because he never said anything about my father or about being on the game to me again. But it was too late, the words had drilled their way inside my head and into my soul, and I would never be able to forget them or to forgive him for uttering them. By saying what he did he showed me what he truly thought of me, reinforcing what I already thought of myself – that I was worthless.

'Prostitute' is a label that the world is quick to attach to somebody, but is never willing to take away. There are so many shades of grey between a woman who allows her lover to keep her financially and a sex worker out on the street picking up kerb-crawlers, but once someone has decided to apply that label everyone is tarred with the same brush. A girl might only ever sell her services once in her entire life, and it might only be a silly mistake made during her teenage years in the course of a drunken night out, but if a newspaper finds out she will always be labelled as 'a prostitute'. Once a woman has made herself vulnerable to such an accusation she has put a skeleton in her closet that anyone can pull out at any time should they want to use it against her. If a partner wants to win a fight, or a newspaper wants to discredit a woman who has gone on to achieve something of public note in later life, that skeleton will always be there, waiting to fall out with a terrible clattering of old bones.

I can never claim that my time on the streets was just a passing phase or a one-off mistake, because Dad kept me out there for years, forcing me to service dozens and dozens of different men. It won't matter what I do with the rest of my life, I will always be known for what happened to me when I was still too young to be able to make my own choices. I was just a child and none of it was my fault; I know that now, but at the moment when Rodney used my past as a weapon to attack me I didn't know that and he made me feel like some piece of dirt he had picked up from the gutter.

At the end of that four-day fight I knew I had to get away before he succeeded in completely destroying me, but he was always there, watching me, threatening me if I dared to disobey him or looked as though I was going near the door. I knew my only chance was to wait until he was asleep in the night, but if he woke up and caught me in the act of leaving I would be in for yet another terrible beating. I suppose it's at moments like that that some abused people give up the fight and hand total victory to their abusers, but to me that seemed a far worse fate than taking a chance. As I lay beside him in bed on the fourth night of that war, I listened to his breathing for hours, my heart pumping adrenaline around my body and keeping me awake despite the fact that my body and my mind were both exhausted from the stress and pain and physical exertion of fighting back for so long. I was trying to work out from the rhythm of his breathing if he was deeply enough under for me to move. Every so often I would try tentatively lifting the duvet as if I was merely turning in my sleep, but he would stir every time I moved and I would freeze again, terrified of bringing him all the way back to the surface.

My mind was buzzing as I lay there, staring into the darkness. If I was going to get out of the house safely I wouldn't be able to stop and pick up Brendan because that would be bound to wake Rodney, and I wouldn't be able to move fast with a baby in my arms. I knew Rodney would never do anything to hurt him and the moment I had reached a safe place I would go to the authorities and get Brendan back, but it was still a painful thought to imagine myself running away from my three-year-old child in the middle of the night, just as Mum had run away from us. At that moment I didn't feel as though I had a choice.

Finally I was able to slip out of the bed without Rodney's breathing pattern changing. My one thought now was to get out of the room without making a sound that would give me away. I tiptoed to the door, terrified that every squeak of the boards would betray me. Out on the landing I gripped the banister and took each step one at a time until eventually I was downstairs. I could still hardly breathe, knowing that if he caught me now I would have no way of explaining convincingly why I had got up and come downstairs. It was only then that I realised I was still in my nightie and hadn't brought down any clothes or shoes with me. There was no way I could go back up without waking him. Looking around I spotted Rodney's work trousers where he had taken them off and dropped them on a chair, and his old denim jacket. I pulled them on over my nightie, tucking it into the waistband of the trousers to make it look like a shirt. There were no shoes anywhere but I was used to going around barefoot and I couldn't delay for a second longer. I opened the door and ran outside into the cold winter night. I was embarrassed to think that other people were going to see me in such a state, but I was also determined that this time Rodney was not going to persuade me to go back to him. I was going to be strong and independent and refuse to accept that I had to take any more beatings just because I was his wife.

I was desperate to think of somewhere I could go where Rodney wouldn't think to look. He knew who all my friends were and he would be quite likely to go banging on their doors if he woke up in the next few minutes or hours and found I was gone. He'd try Mum's straight away, and after that he'd probably call at Chris and Glen's. I racked my brains but finally the only person I could think of who I knew would let me in was Dad. The thought of it made me feel sick, but at least I didn't have Brendan with me. It was like the final straw, the final admission that I had completely failed in life to have to go back to him, but I couldn't think of any alternative and I was too frightened to stay out on the street. I knew Rodney would never think of coming there to look for me and I would find somewhere else to move to the moment the coast was clear in the morning.

Because he still had Terry living with him, I knew Dad's address even though I had never been there. I had seen him around town a few times, but now I was going to be stepping back onto his territory, into the world that he ruled absolutely and in which he had dominated, abused and hurt me for so many years. Although I no longer felt as physically threatened by him as I was by Rodney, I knew that I was walking into a situation where he would be able to demean and humiliate me, making me feel worthless all over again, confirming all my deepest fears about myself. But I had no option. I had to get off the street and into a safe, warm house.

The lights were on and Dad was still up when I got there, just as I thought he would be. My heart was pounding as I tapped nervously on his front door, half of me desperate to turn and run while the other half just wanted to be in off the street before Rodney appeared round the corner.

'Can I come in?' I asked when he opened the door. I couldn't bear to look up at the smug expression that I knew would be on his face as he let me in and saw my bruised and swollen face.

'What's up with you? Husband thrown you out, has he?' I didn't say anything but he realised straight away I was having to turn to him for help just as he always predicted I would have to.

'You are so pathetic,' he gloated. 'What made you think you could ever have a life different to the one you were born for?'

I didn't bother to reply. What was the point? He was right. I was pathetic, at least that was how I felt at that moment, and I needed him to give me shelter.

The moment I was inside the house I knew that nothing at all had changed. All his old friends were strewn around the front room, drinking, and Dad was gloating happily over my downfall. I remembered so many nights as a child being forced to stay awake and drink or play cards with these people or others exactly like them. Dad liked nothing better than being able to fill the house with people who needed him, people who were unable to cope in their own lives for some reason and came to him to give them sanctuary. I suppose it made him feel as though he was some sort of benevolent ruler in his own seedy little kingdom of drug addicts and drunks and women who had been beaten up by their partners or their customers or their pimps. And now I had played completely into his hands by becoming yet another of the waifs and strays who needed him to give them shelter because they had nowhere else to go and no one else to turn to.

'See,' he kept saying as I sat shivering in the corner of the room, waiting for the night to pass. 'I was right. I told you you'd come crawling back. Why don't you just accept it, you can't do anything else? Why don't you just go back to working on the block? It's all you've ever been good for.'

He had a new girlfriend by then, an obese prostitute who kept disappearing upstairs with clients through the rest of the night while Dad and his drunken friends lay around in a semi-comatose state. I felt dirty and pathetic for even being there, believing he was right in everything he said about me and that I was a failure and always would be. All I wanted was for him to be a normal dad and do something to help me get out of the situation I was in, or at least give me some sympathy or advice, but I knew at the same time that it was a hopeless dream and I despised myself for clinging to even that small hope.

Yet at least he had taken me in. Maybe it was true what he had always said when I was younger: 'I'll be there for you, no matter what you do. I'm the only one who will ever truly love you.'

The moment it was light, my first concern was to get Brendan back. I contacted a solicitor I had dealt with before and a few hours later I found myself standing in court, still in the clothes I had escaped in, dramatically sporting two black eyes and a swollen face. The shocking state of my face and my bedraggled outfit must have been enough to convince the judge that I needed his help and he immediately granted me an injunction against Rodney, ordering him not to come within a hundred metres of me. He also evicted him from the house and I was reunited with Brendan by the end of the day. Fired up by my success I remained determined that this time my short-lived marriage was definitely over.

I should have known better, because a week later Rodney and I were back together.

Why do the victims in abusive relationships so often go back to their abusers? It's a question that puzzles many professionals as well as the people themselves. Maybe I had such low esteem that I believed I deserved in some way to be abused, to be unhappy. Maybe that little glimpse of what my life would be like if I fell back into Dad's clutches was enough to frighten me back to Rodney. Couple that with the fact that I knew the children were desperate for us all to be back together and you can see how vulnerable I was likely to be to any pressure Rodney might apply.

He applied plenty from the moment the courts evicted him, mounting a continuous campaign all through the week to convince me that I couldn't cope on my own. My electricity and gas supplies and my telephone line were continually being disconnected from outside the house to make me feel insecure and to make my day-to-day existence too difficult to continue. Whenever I was walking down the road his van would appear from nowhere and he would pull up alongside me. He would be calling out through the open window like the first day we met, completely oblivious to the injunction, begging to be given another chance and promising never to hit me again. I suppose in a way I was flattered that he was willing to put so much time and effort into winning me back, and there was a part of me that wanted to believe him when he said he would change his ways; hope triumphing over experience as usual.

It was also December and I was feeling guilty about ruining Christmas for everyone. The house was already bursting with presents for the kids, making me feel even sadder at the thought of being cut off from the rest of Rodney's family. I wanted to be there to watch their faces when they opened them and to be part of the whole bustle of cooking and drinking and partying. I had been through so many miserable, lonely Christmases as a child both at home and in care, with no presents and absolutely no family to celebrate with, that the festive season meant much more to me than it would do to most adults. It definitely wasn't a time of year when I wanted Brendan to be on his own with me and separated from his sister and brothers. As always Rodney was holding all the cards. Hating myself for my own weakness, I gave in and went back to him.

'Let's have a baby,' he said. 'A baby that's yours and mine, a new part of the family.'

I desperately wanted another baby so I agreed, and I got pregnant almost straight away. During the pregnancy

I convinced myself it was going to be a girl, and that's what Rodney wanted as well because we already had three boys between us. I would be able to brush a little girl's hair and play dollies with her. I was dying to be the mum for her that no one had ever been for me.

Chapter Seven

A New Baby

In 1988, while I was pregnant, Rodney got plenty of work laying 'brick weave' patios and driveways, which he was really good at. He had all the chat and charm to put customers at their ease and make them trust him, and he was never shy of working hard. I was happy to operate the cement mixer, shovelling sand and cement around in order to make paving slabs, or whatever else he needed. I would also do deliveries in the twin-wheeled truck, most of the time with the Brendan in tow, and at the same time I would be working at home cleaning the house, decorating or cooking. It was a full life and kept my mind occupied and the unhappy thoughts and memories at bay for much of the day.

Rodney always had a bunch of friends hanging around him so there were always hordes of people in the house wanting big fry-up breakfasts or dinners in the evenings, all of which I was happy to provide. I loved baking cakes and making puddings and fresh pies and pastries for the kids and any visitors. I felt needed and useful. Maybe it was also a reaction to the many days of hunger that my brother Terry and I had endured as children, when Dad didn't bother to buy any food for us. I never wanted my children to know that feeling and if that meant I spent a large part of the day standing over a hot cooker that was fine by me, even if most of the meals were for the benefit of Rodney's friends.

I guess having an entourage of like-minded men around him, laughing at his jokes, agreeing with everything he said, made Rodney feel better about himself as well. He wasn't the kind of person who liked to be on his own.

One afternoon, while I was heavily pregnant, I was driving through the city centre in the rain and I saw Dad and Terry walking along, both soaked to the skin. My heart was thumping at the thought of having yet more contact with Dad after his gloating attitude when I had turned up on the doorstep last time, but after a brief hesitation I pulled over to offer them a lift. It seemed like the right thing to do for my brother at least, who had never done me any harm and had suffered in many of the same ways as me. I knew that I would feel bad about it if I just drove past and left them, and maybe I felt a little bit empowered because I was driving a car, something that Dad was never able to do. It made me feel like I was the adult in the relationship for once.

They both got in and I tried the best I could to make normal conversation but I felt so flustered and preoccupied with having Dad in the car with me that I was having trouble keeping my thoughts straight. After I dropped them off, I felt strangely pleased with myself for having survived the whole encounter. The torrential rain outside had misted the windows so I didn't realise that Rodney had seen me picking them up until I got home, and found him raging with jealousy. Luckily he didn't hit me because I was pregnant, but to take out his frustrations at my disobedience he grabbed a hammer, stormed out of the house and smashed up the car instead. To do something so irrational suggests that whatever feelings were driving him ran deeper than either of us could imagine.

The baby was due on the 1st of October 1988, when Brendan was three and a half years old. By this time, Mum and I got on quite well as friends, even though I had trouble thinking of her as my mother. Rodney was never going to be the sort of man who would hold my hand and be there for the birth of his child so I asked Mum if she would come along instead. I had asked to give birth at home and Mum was delighted to share in the experience. It was a comfort to have her there, even though I knew I was trying in vain to build a normal mother-daughter relationship with her.

Any disappointment I might have felt when the baby was born and it wasn't a girl was instantly swept away on a wave of euphoria every bit as powerful as the one I had felt when I had Brendan. We called the new baby Thomas and from the start he seemed to me to be just as much of a charmer as his brother had been – although I was more than a little biased, of course.

After Thomas had been born, when I was twenty-one years old, I decided to get sterilised. We now had five kids in the family and I thought that was quite enough. It also occurred to me that if I ever left Rodney for good – which in moments of sad clarity I could see might one day be a possibility – I already had two kids by two different fathers. If I met someone else I would then have three by three different men, and it would start to get ridiculous. Apart from anything else I was entirely happy with my two beautiful boys and with my relationship with our other children. I didn't feel that I would ever need any more in order to feel fulfilled. I didn't want to be stuck on the pill for the rest of my life either. It was surprisingly hard work convincing the doctors to sterilise someone who was not only young but who also seemed to be a pretty good mother. Rodney thought it was a great idea, imagining it would mean more frequent sex for him I guess, although like most men he had no intention of having the snip himself.

It may sound funny to say this, but apart from the episodes of violence and my hatred of the sex, I thought Rodney and I worked well as a partnership. We worked well together and his patios and driveways business was really successful so we did some advertising in Yellow Pages. Because we spent quite a lot of money with them they gave us a free weekend away for two in a hotel down in Felixstowe. We had been working so hard we decided it would be nice to have a break and we set off for our treat in high spirits. It was a weird experience for us suddenly to find ourselves on our own for two days with nothing to do except talk to one another. When we were at home or at work we were always rushed off our feet, surrounded by children or friends or by Rodney's family. Suddenly it was just the two of us with nothing else to distract us, which had never happened before. We hadn't been through the normal process of getting to know each other that other couples experience before they launch themselves into family life, so we had no shared interests or history to fall back on when it was just the two of us.

When you stripped away all the other people in our lives, and all the responsibilities, and put us in a hotel with nothing to do, there was a deafening silence. The only things we could think to talk about were work and the kids. We had no life together as a couple apart from that. There was no intimacy between us. We didn't even know each other very well. There is a photo of me on that weekend, sitting alone, staring into the camera, looking sad and lonely, although I don't think I really realised the full extent of how bad I felt at the time; maybe because I was used to it. We spent most of the weekend on the phone home, checking that everything was going okay without us, and in the end we agreed to cut the weekend short and headed back, both of us eager to return to the life where we were too busy to realise how little we actually cared about one another.

I felt a terrible well of sadness inside me on that drive home, a realisation that I was basically with the wrong man and that the situation was never going to change no matter how much effort we put into the relationship. The fact that I was enjoying many of the aspects of our lives together was as irrelevant as the fact that Rodney had a tendency to hit me when he lost his temper. More important was the fact that I wasn't in love with him and he, despite all the possessiveness, wasn't in love with me. I had a horrible feeling that in the long run what I did feel for Rodney wasn't going to be enough to keep us together through many more difficult times. The older and more independent the children became, the weaker the bonds between us would grow.

Once Thomas had arrived and won my heart, he proved not as easy a child to look after as Brendan had been. He was just as delightful, but altogether more demanding. My strength already diminished by the pregnancy and birth, I found looking after him and helping Rodney to run the business increasingly hard. My nights were frequently sleepless and my throat closed up painfully – something that had happened to me in the past when I was run down and under stress.

The doctor gave me antibiotics but a week later I was back in his surgery, unable even to swallow my own saliva.

'You need to go into hospital,' he told me.

'I can't do that,' I croaked. 'I have a new baby and four other young children to look after.'

He gave me what I guess could be described as an old-fashioned look and said no more. He must have been thinking about my case though, because he turned up unexpectedly at the house later that day and found me in floods of tears, not even able to swallow the medication he had given me that morning. I was no longer strong enough to put up a fight when he insisted I went to hospital and when I got there they immediately put me into isolation while they tried to work out what was wrong. The children weren't even allowed to visit. It seemed as though my own body had decided to turn against me, as if it had decided to give up the fight before my brain or spirit were ready.

The doctors initially diagnosed me with what they called 'a quinsy' (a rare sort of growth in the throat, apparently). In fact, it turned out to be a very severe bout of tonsillitis, but the illness had cashed in on the fact that I was so run down and had grown into something alto-gether more debilitating. They told me that I was anaemic and dehydrated and they hooked me up to a number of drips as they tried to revive my poor, exhausted, battered system.

I realise now that because I had such a low opinion of myself at that time, I wasn't bothering to look after my body properly. I would sometimes go days without eating, once for almost three weeks. As I lay in that hospital bed, slowly feeling the life ebbing back into me from the drips, I had a lot of time to reflect on what I was doing with my life. I knew I was unhappy but the thought of walking away from the family, the one thing I really cared about, was unbearable. I felt completely trapped and despairing.

I had tried to get away from Rodney a few times by now, but every time once my bruises and cuts had healed I would kid myself that the beating hadn't been as bad as I had thought at the time and I would give in to Rodney's campaigns to coax me to stay. But the trouble was there was always another beating on its way within a week or a month, and whenever the next one arrived it instantly reminded me of how bad the ones before had been. Something was going to have to change if I was to survive and find any sort of lasting contentment in my life.

Chapter Eight

The Human Yo-Yo

One evening, after we had all enjoyed a family day out at the Norfolk Show together, I was slow in doing up my seat belt in the car when Rodney told me to. I wasn't rushing because we were still in the car park, crawling at a snail's pace towards the exit as you do at major events like that. Apparently he thought I was being disrespectful or disobedient or both, his temper flared up from nowhere and he punched me repeatedly and so hard on the nose that my blood splattered across the inside of the windscreen before I had a chance to staunch it. The blows went on and on and there was no way to avoid them. The worst part was that the two eldest children were sitting silently in the back watching the whole scene. I couldn't think of anything to say to comfort them because I was too shocked, too dazed by the pain and too busy trying to stop the blood from flowing.

The blood continued to pump out of my nose all the way home, soaking my clothes so there was nothing I could do to hide what had happened from anyone who saw me. When we drew up at the house I froze in my seat. I was too embarrassed to move. I didn't want to get out of the car and have the rest of the world see the state I was in. I was also frightened to go into the house with Rodney in case he was still angry with me and was just waiting till we were behind closed doors to launch another even more ferocious attack. He must have thought I was trying to show him up or make a point by not moving because he bellowed at me to get out of the car immediately.

I moved fast in response to the anger in his voice, some instinctive part of my brain already trained to understand that disobeying him, or even being slow to follow his orders, would result in another beating. I walked straight into the house as quickly as I could, not looking right or left for fear of seeing a neighbour staring, and sat down on the edge of the settee, rigid with fright, unable to work out what I should do next. I was beginning to feel faint from a mixture of the shock, the pain and the loss of blood. There were a couple of Rodney's friends hanging around in the house as usual, but neither of them said a word. They didn't even give me a second glance. It was nothing out of the ordinary to have a blood-soaked woman sitting in the room with you as far as they were concerned.

While I was perched there wondering what to do next, Sue came round with Brendan and Thomas, who she had been looking after for the day. She was shocked to see the state I was in but she obviously guessed immediately what had happened since it had happened to her so often when she was married to Rodney. She made me a cup of tea and helped me to clean myself up. When Rodney walked back in, not realising she was there, Sue let fly at him, giving him a piece of her mind, which ignited his temper all over again and he started shouting at her and ordering her out of his house. Emboldened by having such a vociferous ally, I leapt to her defence and both of us were shouting and screaming at him. At that moment I hated him for what he had done to Sue before me, just as much as she hated him for hitting me now. Even if we couldn't stick up for ourselves with much success, we were good at sticking up for each other, particularly when we were together like this. It amazed me that none of his friends had the courage to speak out about the way Rodney behaved, when the two women he had bullied and tried to beat into submission for so long were prepared to stand up to him.

His pride no doubt dented at being talked back to by mere women, Rodney continued drinking heavily that evening once Sue had gone home with her kids and I was terrified of what would happen to me once his friends had left as well and we were on our own. I knew that as soon as the boys were in bed I needed to get out of the house as quickly as possible. I was certain he would never harm them and I planned to go to the courts to take out an injunction first thing the following day, as I had done before, in order to get him ejected from the house again, this time for good.

I didn't think it would be safe to wait for him to go to bed when he had been drinking so heavily and was already angry with me before Sue and I started having a go and stoked him up even further. So the moment his back was turned I ran out the front door, expecting to hear his footsteps behind me at any moment. My mind was racing even faster than my legs. The first thing I needed was some money. I ran till my lungs felt they were going to burst, all the way to a friend's house. I hammered on the door, gasping for breath as I tried to stress the urgency of my mission, then after borrowing some money I ran on to the local pub to use their phone to call for a taxi. I was struggling to muster enough puff even to get the address out because I was so scared that Rodney was going to appear at any moment. Abandoning that idea, I decided to make my way to the relative safety of the police station nearby. As I ran there, I was expecting at any moment to hear Rodney's van rolling up behind me.

When I finally stumbled through the door and up to the desk, I explained what had happened and that I needed to call a taxi. The Duty Officer was perfectly nice and helpful, but he obviously didn't think that domestic violence was that big a deal. I dare say they got to see any number of cases like mine every day and didn't want to get involved in the paperwork if they could avoid it, knowing that it would never lead to a prosecution. Maybe he knew from experience that women in my position nearly always ended up going back to their husbands in the end, although he was too polite, or too well-trained, to say so.

'Your nose,' he said, staring closely at my face, 'looks like it's broken. You should go down to the hospital and get them to have a look at it.'

I nodded, but I didn't yet feel ready to face more strangers with more questions. I wanted to go somewhere familiar but when the taxi arrived I couldn't think of a single place to tell the driver to take me. I knew I had to think of somewhere, and it had to be a place that Rodney would never think of looking. I couldn't go to Mum's because that would be the first place he would try. In my state of panic, fear and exhaustion the only address I could think of was the one where Dad was living with his new girlfriend. With a sick feeling in my stomach I realised I was going to have to accept defeat and go back there for shelter yet again. It was depressing and humiliating that when it came down to it I couldn't think of anyone else who would protect me. Despite all the times he had told me how worthless I was, and how he was the only person who would ever love me, yet again it looked as if he was right. I was being driven back to him by my lack of options and it felt like the most hopeless situation in the world. Yet again he was going to be able to say that he had been right all along and that I was a miserable failure in life, exactly as he had always told me I was.

I promised myself that I wouldn't stay long, that I just needed somewhere to get away from Rodney while I worked out what to do. I knew my brother Terry was still living with Dad and that he would be there to help me. When I got to the house and knocked it was Dad who answered the door. If he was surprised to see me, or to see the state I was in, he didn't show it.

'Terry's at work,' he told me when I enquired.

'Can I wait for him?' I asked, wanting to get in off the doorstep as quickly as possible in case anyone spotted me.

Dad stood back and I walked through. I smelled the familiar scent of alcohol as I passed him, stirring an unpleasant feeling of nausea in the pit of my stomach. We didn't talk much as I waited for my brother, but enough for Dad to remind me yet again that he had told me I'd be back and to tell me that I was useless and should go back to selling my body down on the block as I was never going to succeed at anything else. I didn't have the strength left for an argument and part of me thought he might be right anyway, so I just sat in silence and listened. As soon as Terry got home from work and saw the state I was in he took me down to the hospital for them to have a look at my nose. They confirmed, as the policeman had suspected, that it was broken and was going to need to be reset.

The next morning vivid bruises had come through to the surface on my face, joining the cuts and swellings, and I looked as though I'd been in a car crash. I had two black eyes and I could hardly speak because my tongue had been split in two and had swollen up to fill my mouth making me feel as if I was about to choke. It was impossible to eat anything and hard to even drink without a straw. I went straight to court as soon as I woke up to ask them to remove Rodney from the house so that I could go back to my kids, as I had in the past. Even though I was standing in front of him with the evidence of Rodney's violence written all over me, the judge still refused to do anything until he had heard Rodney's side of the story. I couldn't believe what I was hearing.

He adjourned the case for two weeks, but he did at least grant me an injunction against Rodney so that he couldn't come near me, although I knew from experience how little notice he was likely to take of that, and he did grant me custody of the boys, which was the most important thing to me at that stage. I had sought the help of the courts before and I wonder if they were beginning to look at my record and think I was wasting their time. Maybe they thought there was no point going to too much trouble on my behalf because I would always end up going back to him. As long as the children were safe they could just wait a couple of weeks and everything would sort itself out. But this time I was more determined to stay away than I had ever been before. This had been by far the worst beating Rodney had ever given me, in terms of the amount of damage he had caused, and he didn't seem to feel any remorse for it.

I appealed to him directly to get out of the house and let the boys and me stay there until the hearing but he refused point blank. I suppose he thought I would be going back to him sooner or later, and if he kept hold of the house it was more likely to be sooner. It was as if he thought beating me was a perfectly reasonable thing to do, certainly not something that was worth making all this fuss about. From my point of view the fact that he had done it in front of the children made it much worse. This wasn't the sort of world I wanted my boys growing up in, however much they might love their dad. I didn't want them to believe it was an acceptable way for any man to behave towards any woman.

My initial problem was finding somewhere for the boys and me to stay until the courts got round to evicting Rodney from the house. By this stage I had managed to develop quite a close relationship with my mum, thanks in many ways to Rodney bringing us together so often, inviting her round for barbecues and Sunday dinners and the rest, and so I turned to her. I was terrified that she would turn us away, fulfilling all my worst fears about the reality of our relationship and making me feel rejected all over again. But instead she offered to let us stay for the two weeks until the case went back to court, after which I was sure I would be able to get back into the house.

'My God,' she said when she first saw my face later that day. 'You look like you've been in a car crash. I'm never speaking to that man again after what he's done to you.'

Letting us stay with her was a lifesaver of an offer, although I have to say I never felt exactly comfortable or at home in her house. When I go round to some of my friends' houses I always feel completely relaxed about things like helping myself to a cup of coffee if I want one, but I would never have felt I could do that at Mum's. All the same, we did normal family things like shopping, cooking meals and washing up, and we did all the normal chores that we had never done together when I was small. We spent a lot of that fortnight talking, more like two friends than like a mother and daughter. She was very open about her time with Dad and told me about how he had forced her onto the streets and what a disastrous relationship they had had. I felt I could talk to her about anything, which might not have been the case if I had thought of her as more of a mother figure. It felt good to find some common ground, even if it was an unfortunate situation.

About a week after I got there I was coming home from a visit to my solicitor one afternoon and saw Rodney's truck parked outside the house. Angry that he was daring to invade the place where I was seeking sanctuary from him, but not really surprised that he was ignoring the court injunction as usual, I strode into the house, feeling empowered and fully prepared to chuck him out. When I got inside I found him and Mum sitting down in the front room, sharing a cup of coffee as if it was the most normal thing in the world. There was a massive bunch of red roses waiting on the table, which I picked up and shoved straight into the bin.

'Rodney's been saying how sorry he is about everything,' Mum told me, 'and about how much he loves you.'

I couldn't believe that he had been able to win her over to his side so quickly when just a week before she had been saying she would never speak to him again because of what he had done to me. In the heat of the moment it seemed to me that she was betraying me, taking his side against me, and I jumped to the conclusion that it was because she wanted to get us out of her house as quickly as possible. I had been feeling guilty about imposing on her, but at the same time there was a tiny part of me that enjoyed the thought that I finally had a mother who was willing to take care of me when I needed it. Now it felt as though the whole set-up had been a sham and she hadn't meant any of the things she'd said. Maybe she had even been intending to win me back for Rodney from the start.

I made it very clear that I had no intention of going back to him and sent him on his way, before laying into

Mum for her treachery. If I had had anywhere else I could have gone I would have marched out with the boys then and there, but as usual I was trapped once more by a lack of options.

I think it was difficult for both Mum and me to judge whether a man was good or bad. We could appreciate the fact that it was wrong to hit a woman, but that is easy to forget when the bruises have healed and they are professing their undying love for you and promising that it will never happen again. If the option is loneliness, or falling back into the power of a man like my father, then it becomes all too easy to believe their promises.

After two weeks the law took its course and Thomas, Brendan and I were back in our own home without Rodney, although Rodney didn't let up on his campaign to persuade me to take him back for even a day. I held out for a whole month before weakening and letting him back in this time. I wanted so much for our family to be back together again. To anyone watching my progress through life from the outside, it must all have looked so predictable and so pathetic. However much he abused and beat me I would go back to him and then he would beat and abuse me again.

There was a gap of a few months before he next hurt me, but subconsciously I must have known it was going to happen because this time I had prepared somewhere to go so that I didn't have to rely on either of my parents. I had recently got back in touch with a friend called Mel who I had been with in a children's home called Break back when I was twelve. She lived miles away, up near Liverpool, and knew all about my situation with Rodney because I had told her everything on the phone. She had said I could stay with her if I ever needed a sanctuary, and Liverpool seemed a nice safe distance away, too far for him to pop round for a cup of tea with a bunch of roses.

The next beating happened on Thomas's first birthday and reminded me yet again that I had to find the strength to break away from the cycle of violence because it was never going to end as long as I stayed with Rodney. I took my time, laying my plans more carefully than before, and it was the following day when I phoned Mel. She told me to bring the boys up to stay with her and it felt as though I finally had a chance of starting a new life for all three of us in a new city, well out of Rodney's reach. He knew nothing about Mel and wouldn't be able to find me in order to pester me and persuade me to come back. I told myself that this time I was making the final break. I took it calmly, not running out into the night in my bare feet or hurtling out of the front door with no idea where I was going. I waited till Rodney had gone off to work then I quickly packed a few things, having banked a cheque from the business so we would have a bit of money to start us off. I kept an ear out for Rodney all the time I was preparing the boys, ready to cover my tracks in an instant if he came back unexpectedly. It was his habit to go out to work early but then he might pop back unannounced from time to time during the day to check up on me. I had no idea how long I had.

I didn't feel guilty about taking money from the business because this time I was leaving Rodney with a nice, well-furnished, three-bedroom house, all the vehicles and the business itself. I didn't intend to ask him for another penny because I wanted to prove to myself as much as anyone else that I was capable of standing on my own feet without a man to support me. In fact he was going to come out of the break-up a lot better off than I was, but that didn't bother me in the least. I just wanted to make a new start. I had worked hard for him and never taken a wage, so it felt as though it was my money anyway.

Finally ready, I called for a taxi to take us to the station. They told me it would just be a few minutes. I brought our bags down to the hall so we would be ready when it arrived. When I looked up, I came face to face with Rodney. I had been distracted at the last moment and hadn't seen or heard him coming, so there was no time to hide the bags or make out I was doing something else. He saw me standing there, with all my possessions packed around me, Brendan beside me and Thomas in my arms, and knew instantly what I was planning.

There was a horrible frozen moment as we both stared at each other. I was sure he was going to attack me and beat me to a pulp yet again in front of the kids, but I couldn't think how to get them out of the way in time. He lunged at me and I wasn't able to move quickly enough to stop him from grabbing Thomas. Instinctively I tightened my grip on my baby so he wouldn't be torn from my arms, but Rodney kept pulling. This grotesque tug-of-war probably only went on for a couple of seconds but I suddenly saw us as if I were looking from the outside, literally tearing our own baby apart. As we stretched him, Thomas set up a terrible screaming. I could see Rodney wouldn't let go so I was going to have to.

Rodney had always been a brilliant father to Brendan and the others, but from the moment Thomas was born he had seemed to be his father's favourite. We all knew it and accepted it.

'You can take your little bastard,' he shouted, gesturing at Brendan who was watching the whole thing with a look of shell-shocked horror on his face, 'but you will never take Thomas.'

He was banking on my maternal instincts being too strong to allow me to walk away from my baby in cold blood. I felt as though I was being torn in half, just like Thomas. On the one hand, Mel's offer seemed like my last chance of escaping and starting a new life for myself and the boys. If I let this opportunity slip through my fingers, who knew when I would get another? Rodney had no idea where Mel lived, and he didn't know I had the money I needed to support myself until I found a job and got on my feet. He was holding Thomas now and staring me down, daring me to even think of trying to snatch him back. Over his shoulder I could see that the taxi had arrived outside the house. This was my last chance. I had to make a snap decision. If I stayed I would certainly get another beating and Rodney would be watching me even more carefully, so I might not get another chance for months. But I knew I wasn't going to be able to get Thomas off him now – I couldn't risk hurting him in the struggle that was bound to ensue – so I would have to steel myself to walking out without him. I had always been able to get the courts to help me get the kids back before, so I had to assume they would do it for me again.

I made my decision. Taking Brendan firmly by the hand I grabbed my bags and ran for the taxi, leaving Rodney shouting after me with our baby gripped tightly in his arms. Even though I was sure I would be able to get Thomas back within a few days I still felt I was deserting him, doing to him exactly what Mum had done to us. I had to force my legs to keep going, like in a nightmare, reminding myself that Mum had vanished completely and never made any attempt to contact us or get us back, which I had no intention of doing. This separation would not last for a second longer than it had to. On the way to the station in the taxi I had to try to hold everything together so as not to frighten Brendan by bursting into tears, but inside I felt as though my heart was breaking.

It was a six-hour rail journey to Mel's, which gave me an awful lot of time to think about Thomas and everything else I was leaving behind. I might have been miserable for most of my life in Norwich but it had still been my home since the day I was born and this was the first time I had ever ventured out into the wider world. The distance to Liverpool had seemed a good thing when I had been planning to get away from Rodney, but now that the miles we were covering were taking me away from my baby it felt very different. Every minute seemed like an age. I wondered if this was how Mum had felt the day she left us. I had gone and done the one thing I had always sworn I wouldn't do: I had left my child. I could understand how Mum had come to feel that she had no other choice, but in my heart I knew I would get Thomas back. I certainly wouldn't have left the house that day if I hadn't been certain of that. I also knew that Rodney would never harm him, whereas Mum had known Dad wasn't fit to be left in sole charge of children. She had told social services about his boasts that he would make me the best little prostitute on the block and yet they still failed to protect me from him. Rodney was nothing like Dad in that respect. He might be a bit old-fashioned and harsh in his views on child-rearing, but he was still a good father.

As soon as I got to Mel's I went to see a solicitor in order to get the ball rolling. He listened and nodded wisely as I poured out my story and his expression was grave.

'The problem is,' he said eventually, 'that you are the one who has left the child. The courts wouldn't look on that favourably.'

The terrible sick feeling intensified in the pit of my stomach. Had I made a mistake? Had I played straight into Rodney's hands? Was crawling back to him going to be the only way I would get Thomas back?

'Do you have reason to believe Thomas is in any danger from his father?' the solicitor asked.

'No,' I shook my head. I could never have said that I believed Rodney would do anything to harm his favourite son, however much I might want to in order to get Thomas back. 'If I had been concerned about that I would never have left him.'

'In that case …' the solicitor spread his hands as if to show that he believed the cause was already lost and there was nothing he could do to help me.

'So, what are my chances of getting Thomas back?' I asked, aware that my voice was cracking.

'I think it is unlikely,' he replied kindly, 'unless you physically kidnap him.'

I didn't know what to do, but I did know I wasn't going to do anything like that. The boys were the most important people in my life and I wasn't going to do anything that might put either of them in danger. I didn't want to admit defeat and go back to Norwich, but although Mel was being a wonderful friend I also knew that I couldn't expect her to have Brendan and me in her house forever.

After leaving the solicitor's office I headed to the council to see if I could get them to house me. I had to do something to make myself feel less helpless and maybe, I reasoned, I would stand a better chance of having Thomas returned to me if I had a home of my own to take him to.

'How long have you been living in this area?' the council worker asked as I told him what I wanted.

'I've just arrived,' I said. 'I had to run away from a violent relationship.'

'I'm sorry,' he said, although he didn't look it. 'You have to have been here in Liverpool for six months before you become eligible for housing.'

Unable to think what to do for the best I stayed with Mel for two weeks in a horrible state of limbo. It should have been the start of a wonderful new life of freedom, but every hour of the day I was missing Thomas and racking my brains, trying to think of a way to get him away from Rodney without doing him any further damage. But it seemed hopeless when I didn't even have a proper home to bring him back to. I was constantly thinking about him and imagining what he would be doing at that exact moment and knowing I should be back home with him, taking care of his needs like a proper mum. It felt completely unnatural and wrong for any mother to be so far away from a one-year-old baby.

After two weeks I couldn't bear the separation a moment longer and I had to admit that Rodney had defeated me yet again. I had to get back to Thomas and there was no other way. I rang Rodney and asked him to come and fetch us. I have still never really forgiven myself for those two weeks that I was apart from Thomas, and at the same time I despised myself for being so weak and allowing myself to be drawn back into the endless destructive, repetitive cycle. I felt even more worthless and disempowered than I had before this latest attempt at freedom. What use was I to the children if I kept on giving in like this? What kind of mother was I?

Chapter Nine

An Escape Route

Over the coming years, while accepting that I wasn't able to escape, I made several attempts at building an independent life for myself while staying within the marriage and the family, so that I wasn't completely under Rodney's thumb all day and every day. I eventually talked him into letting me do a couple of part-time jobs: one was cleaning and another was working in a hospital taking round meals and refreshments to the patients, which I really enjoyed. None of these jobs ever lasted long, though, because Rodney hated me having any sort of independence and would always make things difficult for me, using guerrilla tactics such as turning up too late when he was due to babysit, so I wasn't able to get to work on time. He couldn't actually stop me from taking the jobs, but he made it as hard as he could for me to keep them, constantly moaning because I wasn't there for him or the children when he felt I should be. He did, however, make a concession that I could go to bingo once a week with Sue and a group of friends and neighbours, although even then he would sometimes come back home late on purpose so that I couldn't go because that would have meant leaving the children on their own.

'I'd really like to go back to college and get some more education,' I told him several times, but he just laughed at the idea.

'Why would you want to do that?' he wanted to know. 'I can give you everything you need. Why can't you be happy with the life you've got? Why do you have to keep pining for more?'

In one way I could see what he meant. Was I being ungrateful? Compared to the lifestyle Dad had forced on me everything about my life now was wonderful. Should I just shut up and get on with it as Rodney said? Most of the time I did that, but the unhappiness and the lack of fulfilment kept on nagging away inside me, wearing me down. Rodney had laid down so many rules – like the ones that said I wasn't allowed to wear skirts or make-up because that would mean I was having an affair – that it was too much effort to fight every one of them. It was easier just to give in on the ones that didn't really seem to matter, rather than risk taking a beating and having to give in eventually anyway. The only other option was to walk out again and go through the whole charade once more.

His jealousy and insecurity about me never seemed to abate as the years passed. He had no reason ever to doubt that I was always faithful to him, but that didn't stop him from beating up any man who he thought was showing too much interest in me, or of accusing me of having affairs with any man I ever spoke to. Even though I didn't love him I would never have been unfaithful to him because I respected him and he was my husband. He knew I hated having sex anyway, so why would he think I would go deliberately looking for more of it? If there was one thing my father's fickle lifestyle had instilled in me, it was the need to believe that people who had made a commitment to one another should always stick to their word and be loyal to one another, especially if there were children involved. The way Dad had treated Mum, despite the fact that he always claimed she was the love of his life, had been the root cause of everything that had gone wrong for my brothers and me during our child-hoods and I would never have dreamed of doing anything like that to our children. I despised infidelity.

Twenty-six seems to be some sort of magical age for the women in our family. Mum was twenty-six when she left Dad, Sue was the same age when she left Rodney, and so was I.

I suppose what made this escape plan the one that worked was partly to do with my own growing self-confidence and partly to do with the fact that this time I had somewhere sensible to take the boys. Rodney and I had exchanged our lovely council house for a flat because we no longer felt we needed the expense of a whole house. In 1991 we had moved into a mobile home that was parked in the grounds of a dilapidated garden centre and restaurant, which we had started running as a business. We kept the council flat, though, just in case anything went wrong with the business, but we had no immediate plans to use it.

The guy who had owned the garden centre before us had let it all go to pieces after his wife left him, so there was a lot of potential for improvement. Our main line of business at that stage was making concrete garden ornaments and paving slabs, so the site suited us perfectly. We also managed to take advantage of a government enterprise allowance scheme which helped people starting their own businesses and we were soon up and running.

Although the old garden centre seemed to be a great opportunity for a young family to start with, living in the mobile home proved to be more of a challenge than I had expected. There was so little space it had to be kept scrupulously tidy and even then we all got under each other's feet. The children loved it, though. In some ways it was an idyllic, semi-wild existence. The mobile was parked in a sheep field belonging to Gordon, the farmer next door, with whom we became firm friends, and we had a nanny goat that would wake us at six each morning, bleating to be milked. Rodney would do that job and would come back in with warm goats' milk for the children to pour over their breakfast cereals. In the spring the children were able to watch the lambing and Fred would help bottle-feed the weak ones that had been rejected by their mothers. Rodney was full of money-making ideas for the place, including starting up a clay pigeon shoot in partnership with Gordon. We even had our own aviary complete with a peacock.

Gordon and his wife Molly were well known in the local villages and used to run a charity fun day on the field at the back of the garden centre, which we became very involved with, helping out with things like the catering and the donkey derby. A few weeks after the event we were all invited to a nearby pub for the handing over of the cheque to the charity. It was a nice evening but the more I relaxed and talked to people the more jealous and possessive Rodney became. There was a lot of hugging, back-slapping and cheek kissing, which made him increasingly agitated as he glowered across the bar at me. Eventually he decided he'd had enough and marched me out of the pub and pushed me into the front seat of the estate car we were driving at the time. I was upset because I didn't know what I had done wrong and it was one of the rare occasions when we had the chance of a pleasant evening out in nice company.

Rodney took no notice of my protests, climbing into the driving seat and roaring off angrily, shouting accusations at me, telling me I had been flirting – which I hadn't been because I would never have dared. I knew I was going to get a beating as soon as we got home and I was desperate to escape. Even though the car was going at fifty miles an hour I tried to open the door and get out, but Rodney held me firmly in my seat without even slowing down. Determined to escape his grip I wriggled free and climbed over into the back. I tried the doors again but they had child locks on and Rodney was in control. My mind still set on getting as far from his fists as possible, I climbed over the back seats and into the hatchback boot area. There was a jack lying on the floor. I picked it up and started smashing it against the side window, sending splinters of glass flying out behind the car.

Obviously wanting to get me home as quickly as possible so he could get his hands on me, Rodney didn't take his foot off the accelerator. I didn't care what happened next as long as I escaped. Once I'd smashed a big enough hole in the window I pushed my way through it. As soon as Rodney realised what I was doing he slammed on the brakes but it was too late and I was already landing on the tarmac of the main road, knocking the breath out of my body. Unable to move for a few moments, I lay still, trying to work out what damage I had done to myself.

I hadn't managed to escape him because he immediately came charging back to pick me up and I was in no shape to run away, but I had at least succeeded in stunning him out of his anger. He helped me back into the car. By some miracle, it seemed I hadn't broken any bones, although I looked a terrible mess of grazes and bruises. I think we were both shocked by the thought of what had nearly happened, all because of a silly drunken row. I spent most of the next day picking shards of glass and bits of tarmac out of my arms and legs.

I didn't leave that day or the next, but the incident was one of the final nails in the coffin of our relationship.

The restaurant in the garden centre had done well in the past, mainly catering for coach parties, so we gave it a lick of paint and started providing scones and afternoon teas, and then we went on to do Sunday dinners. All through the summer of 1992 it was a success and word started to spread. We introduced tea dances and discos in the evenings for coach parties and holidaymakers, hiring chefs and waitresses and all the rest of the support staff needed for a growing enterprise. Local people began to take an interest in what we were doing as well and a man called John started coming in with his wife to eat. He seemed a romantic-looking figure to me: tall, long-haired and slim, and he rode a motorbike. He told us that as well as being a mechanic he was also a disc jockey and asked if he could work with us. We took him on and he became our resident DJ as well as our friend.

John was a couple of years younger than me and right from the beginning he was really sweet to me, paying me compliments in a way that would never have occurred to Rodney. One night he told me I had 'beautiful green eyes' and his words almost knocked me off my feet. No one had ever complimented me before – quite the opposite. I was used to being told how fat and ugly I was by Dad, and that I was useless and no one would ever love me except him. The only time Rodney would say anything even faintly romantic was when he was drunk and wanted sex. Our relationship had grown no more intimate with the years than it had been on our ill-fated weekend in Felixstowe. He would certainly never have agreed to dance with me or anything like that. In fact, the one time I asked him to dance he just laughed, as if it was the most stupid suggestion he had ever heard, apparently not noticing that he left me feeling hurt, rejected and humiliated.

My friend Jane came over to visit around that time and she talked a lot about her relationship with her husband. Among other things, she told me that he would wash and condition her hair for her, which amazed me. She said he even shaved her legs for her. Did men really do that sort of thing for their partners? It wasn't something I could imagine Rodney ever doing for me, not in a million years.

If you have never been paid compliments before it is hard not to react when you are told you have 'beautiful green eyes' and I'm sure it was obvious to anyone who was watching me that John had hit a chord. It got to the stage where I didn't even dare to look at him and I would get into a complete dither when I was around him. It was not so much because of him, as because he made me realise I could easily meet someone with whom I could fall in love and who would love me in the way I wanted to be loved. I was nervous that Rodney would start accusing me of having an affair with John if he saw me talking to him or looking at him too much. I couldn't be sure that such an accusation wouldn't make me blush in a way that would make me appear distinctly guilty.

Despite the care I thought I was taking, I must have been more transparent than I thought because other friends commented on the chemistry between John and me, which made me even more nervous that someone might say something in Rodney's hearing. If the same thought occurred to Rodney, he would be certain to beat John up without stopping to ask questions first.

Although it was nice having John around the place, I never dreamed for a moment that it would develop into anything since we were both married and he knew my views on infidelity. Although I didn't believe there could ever be anything between us, the fact that I enjoyed his company so much more than Rodney's terrified me. It made me realise even more strongly that by staying married to Rodney I was living a lie. I had kept it up for eight years by that stage, but I wasn't sure how much longer I could go on doing it for the sake of the family unit.

A group of people who worked for us or hung around at the restaurant knew that John was having problems in his marriage because late one night, after the disco had finished, he had told us that he was thinking of leaving his wife. He was obviously deeply troubled by the prospect of letting her down, and to add to his problems she had just discovered she was pregnant. He asked us what we thought he should do, and we all told him he should have thought about whether he wanted to stay with her before he got her pregnant.

'Why should I make myself miserable for the rest of my life,' he wanted to know, 'just because she's having a child?'

'What a bastard!' we all agreed once he had left for the night.

At the same time as disapproving of what John was thinking of doing in his private life, I was becoming more and more depressed at the thought of the loveless life that stretched ahead of me in my own marriage. I was also becoming increasingly concerned that Brendan and Thomas might grow up believing that it was all right for a man to hit a woman because they had seen Rodney hitting me so often and had also seen that I kept coming back and staying around to let him do it again, which was as good as condoning it. It wasn't just the physical violence that I thought was a bad influence on them either; I didn't want them to grow up believing that it was right for men to dominate and control the women in their lives, treating them almost like possessions rather than people.

I decided that I had to do something decisive before it was too late and this was the perfect opportunity as we still had the council flat in Norwich. It even had furniture in it because we hadn't been able to move everything to the mobile home. I could easily move the boys back there because they were still enrolled at the local school and would be able to slot back into their previous lives with hardly any disruption. It wouldn't be like carting them all the way to Liverpool. I knew that Rodney loved living in the mobile home, so I didn't have to feel guilty about that. I made the decision. It was time to act.

My friend Jane came over to help me pack up while Rodney was out and we crammed the boys, the family dog and all our most vital worldly possessions into the back of her estate car. On the way into Norwich we stopped for petrol at the garage where John worked. He wasn't there so I scribbled a note to him, thanking him for his friendship, wishing him all the best for his future and hoping it all worked out okay for him. I didn't want him to think I had just vanished into thin air without telling him. Even though I knew we had a lot in common because he was going through a tough time with his marriage too, I didn't give him any details about how to contact me. I think I wanted to leave behind everything to do with my life with Rodney and the garden centre, which meant all the other people who were connected to it as well, including John. After writing the note and filling up the car, we headed on with the journey into our new future.

I didn't expect to hear from John again, although I knew I would always have fond memories of the kind things he had said to me and be grateful for the contribution they had made to me finding the confidence necessary to make the break and go out looking for something better in life. That evening, however, to my complete surprise, the phone in the flat rang and when I picked up it was John's voice on the other end.

'Can we meet for a drink?' he asked.

I didn't answer for a moment, shocked that he had found me so easily – I think he had called Jane and wormed it out of her – and also by how pleased I felt to hear from him. At the same time the thought of Rodney finding out that I had met John and believing that that was the reason why I had left him terrified me. I had seen what Rodney could do to someone who did no more than look at me strangely, so I dreaded to think what he would do to a man he thought had stolen his wife. The funny thing was that many of Rodney's friends had made passes at me at one time or another, but Rodney never found out about any of them. I would never have dreamed of taking up any of their offers because I respected Rodney too much, and because he was my husband, but I had become increasingly disillusioned over the years with these men who called themselves his friends. I suppose Rodney must have been behaving in just the same way with other women when I wasn't around.

I didn't intend to get into a new relationship at all for a while, believing I needed time to recover from everything that had happened and to decide what direction I wanted my life to go in before I even thought about the complications of another man. And since I still hated sex there was no immediate temptation to go rushing off after anyone new anyway.

'Just as friends,' John said, 'obviously.'

When he put it like that it seemed churlish to turn him down. It would sound as if I thought I was so irresistible he wouldn't be capable of just being my friend. So I agreed and a few days later we met up for a drink. The moment we were together it was obvious to both of us that there was already something more between us than friendship. We both fell hopelessly in love, but to me there seemed no chance that we could ever do anything about it since I knew his wife was pregnant and I didn't want to set Rodney against him. It all just seemed too complicated to work. I actually felt guilty about the strength of my feelings for him. Not only was he a married man, albeit an unhappy one, but he was also about to be a father. How could we possibly start an affair under those circumstances? The idea of 'just being friends', however, was becoming harder and harder to contemplate once I realised I was falling in love with him.

Despite the fact that I had the flat and the boys to keep me occupied, it was still hard going back to living on my own again after having been so much part of Rodney's world. I liked the idea of having John around to provide moral support, but at the same time I didn't really want the complications of having another man in my life. I wanted to get on with sorting the boys out at school and getting away from Rodney once and for all before starting anything new. I was also enjoying the freedom of being able to go out when I wanted to without having to answer to Rodney, and being able to wear a bit of make-up or a skirt if I felt like it. I'd never really been to clubs before because Rodney wasn't interested in any of that, but I loved to dance and drink and let myself go.

After so many years of treading on eggshells for fear of upsetting first my father and then my husband, I went a bit mad in those early months of my separation. In my rush to forget all my worries and guilt and to enjoy my newfound freedom to the full I started taking a lot of speed again, as I had when I was a teenager working the streets or living in care homes. I had given up all drugs while I was with Rodney and trying to be a good mother to the kids, but now I was on my own again I found it helped to accentuate the joys of the moment and block out the dark side of my thoughts while I partied. Perhaps I was trying to make up for the years I felt I had lost while I was with Rodney, who would never have anything to do with recreational drugs. I had gone almost straight from being a child to being a mother of five and now I wanted to enjoy the bit of my life that would normally have come in between those two stages. The only trouble was that I threw myself into the wildness a bit too whole-heartedly. I was running out of control and totally losing the plot. It was inevitable that there was going to be a crash.

Chapter Ten

Breakdown

John finally left his wife shortly after I left Rodney and moved into lodgings on his own. Although I knew for sure that I loved him, I didn't respect what he had done or the way he was treating his wife and unborn child, and that made me disgusted with myself for the way I felt about him. Although Rodney had his faults, there was no denying how family-orientated he was; he would never have left a pregnant wife. Inevitably other people found out that John and I were seeing each other and most of them jumped to the conclusion that was why we had both left our marriages, which made me feel even worse, partly because I could see the way I was behaving and I didn't much like it.

Rodney still knew nothing about my feelings for John, or even that we were seeing each other, and he didn't seem to be particularly bothered that I had left him this time. I had done it so many times in the past he was obviously convinced that I would see the error of my ways and come back in due course, just as I had always done in the past. He wasn't in any hurry, like an old cat watching the mouse scurrying around in front of him, waiting for the right moment to pounce. Maybe he thought that no one else would show an interest in me now that I was a bit older and the mother of two growing boys, or, knowing how much I hated sex, maybe he assumed that I wouldn't want a relationship with anyone else.

When he did finally discover that I was seeing John, and heard that John had left his wife despite her pregnancy, Rodney's attitude changed overnight and he went ballistic. He immediately assumed that we must be more than 'just friends'. As far as he was concerned the initial period of amnesty was over. John and I started receiving threats of violence and nuisance phone calls. I ignored it all to start with, putting it down to bluster, until there was an anonymous call in which a man threatened the boys' lives. I could no longer take the risk that it was just Rodney's mates trying to show him how tough they were and dismiss it as bluff. The police and the school had to be involved, our letterbox had to be sealed because there had been talk of petrol bombs being delivered to the flat, and I started to feel very afraid that I had put my children's lives in danger with my actions.

Rodney and John came to blows a few times after that, and so did John's wife and I. Understandably, she thought the break-up of her marriage was all my fault. In those circumstances it is virtually impossible to convince any woman that her husband was planning to leave her anyway and that the woman he is now seeing was nothing to do with the decision. Everyone wants to believe that there is someone out there they can blame for their misfortunes.

John found himself being harassed on his way to work on his motorbike, repeatedly forced off the road by trucks that seemed to be being driven by homicidal maniacs. Or he would find that his motorbike battery had been stolen or his tyres let down in the night. It was a terrible time for all of us and there was no escaping that fact; all we could do was live through the turmoil and hope it eventually calmed down. We never found out who was responsible for the threats – or whether the timing was just a coincidence. I remained resolute in my decision that my marriage was over and I was not going back to Rodney, no matter how much pressure he piled on. John and I kept deciding not to see each other in order to give everyone time to calm down, but neither of us was able to go through with it and within a few days one of us would be calling the other. We were still telling ourselves that we were just good friends, both in need of a sympathetic ear, and that we weren't doing anything wrong, when in our hearts we knew that wasn't the case.

The worst part of breaking up with Rodney for me was having to leave his other children. I had been an integral part of their lives for eight years and I knew that they felt I had walked out on them. I could remember all too clearly and painfully what that felt like from my own childhood. They seemed more upset by the changes than Brendan and Thomas were and they made it obvious that they wanted me to go back. I could understand how they felt because of my own experiences. Even though I hadn't disappeared completely in the way my mother had, and still got to see them because we were living in the same city, it could never be the same as when we were all one family. No child wants to lose people from their close family group, especially if they are happy with the ways things are. Although we all remained on very good terms, I don't think they ever truly forgave me and I have to accept that because I know I never forgave my mum either.

There was so much to think about and worry about during those months that the pressures were building inside my head. To be honest, I had still never had a chance to deal with everything that had happened to me as a child. I had gone from being abused by my father and sold to men for sex, to struggling to survive in the care system, and straight from there to teenage mother-hood and then marriage to a man who thought nothing of hitting me and controlling every aspect of my life. I had responsibility for two little boys when I still hadn't lived out my own childhood. On top of all that I was now feeling guilty about leaving my husband and for falling in love with a man who had just left his pregnant wife. It was at this moment that my mind gave up the unequal struggle and I slid into a nervous breakdown, no longer able to cling on under the pressure.

My GP had been trying to make me take anti-depressants to get me through the difficult times, but I wouldn't listen to his advice. Anti-depressants would probably have helped but at the same time, maybe avoiding any mind-numbing medication forced me to deal head-on with the many demons that were now rising to the surface, rather than allowing me to ignore them in a pharmaceutically induced fog.

The sensitive way in which John handled my descent into near-madness blew me away. There was no way Rodney would have been willing to put up with what he would have seen as foolish figments of my imagination. He would just have told me to pull myself together and get on with life, which was more or less what I had been doing during the eight years that I had spent with him: repressing every emotion, denying that there was anything wrong, bottling up the misery.

John came from a normal, decent family, completely different from anything I had known, but still he seemed to understand what I was going through better than anyone else I had ever met. When I thought about how other people must see me I felt wretched. Apart from the sordid details of my abused childhood and my time as an underage streetwalker, I was now a single mum with two children by different men. I was also taking recreational drugs, especially speed, and drinking far more than I should have done, telling myself that I was just enjoying my newfound freedom when in fact I was probably trying to escape from everything that was going on in my life, desperately trying to drown out the many voices shouting inside my head. Another reason to drink was that it allowed me to lose all my inhibitions, but the downside of that was that it also allowed all the demons that I kept repressed inside me to come bursting to the surface, which was not always an attractive sight.

Ridiculously, the more John professed his love for me the angrier I became with him because I didn't know how to deal with the affection and I was certain I wasn't good enough for him. Wasn't that what Dad had always told me? 'No one will ever love you except me.' So, I reasoned, John must be lying when he told me he loved me.

'You'll leave me one day,' I would shout at the poor man whenever he tried to express his feelings for me. 'Everyone leaves me or abuses me in the end.'

I would work myself into a state and convince myself that I didn't trust him, until I couldn't listen to reason. Every time I'd had too much to drink, I'd go over and over the same territory, yelling about all the reasons why he should leave me and go back to his wife. At the same time I wanted to be good enough for him so that I could believe that we could live happily ever after; I just didn't think it was possible. I was certain that I would end up being hurt and disappointed again if I allowed myself to become vulnerable. I wanted to protect myself but I had no idea how to do it.

'We'll get married one day,' he would say, patiently trying to soothe me as I ranted on. 'And then everything will be all right.'

Partly because I was drinking and taking speed, and partly because of the emotional turmoil I was going through, I lost two stone in weight within six months of leaving Rodney. It felt as if the teenager had been let loose in me again, as if I had been given permission to be myself but, like so many teenagers who go off the rails, I had no idea who I was, what I wanted or even what I liked. I was obsessed with John, but at the same time I was longing for the safety and security of being back with Rodney who, I guess, had in many ways been a father substitute to me. At the same time as wanting to let my hair down and enjoy myself at every opportunity, I was also aware that I needed to be a responsible mother to the boys.

During my eight years with Rodney I had been so preoccupied with our relationship, with the family and children and our various business ventures, that I hadn't had time to dwell on the past and the traumas of my childhood. That had probably been part of the attraction – keeping myself busy to avoid facing the issues that still lurked in the hidden recesses of my memory. Now that I was free to think about stuff I hadn't had time for before, everything seemed to bring back memories I was most frightened of remembering.

Only once I had moved into the flat full-time, for instance, did I notice that it was next door to a block where Dad had lived for a while during my childhood and that the layout of the rooms was exactly the same as I remembered from the past. The moment I had spotted that it freaked me out completely, filling my mind with hideous pictures and voices and memories of fear, pain, humiliation and unhappiness. There were times when I believed I could actually smell my father's stale, alcohol-soaked breath as if it was on my face again, inescapable as he smothered me with his lust, filling my mouth and nostrils. I would suddenly remember details from the past like the candy-striped sheets on his bed. Then I remembered how he used to try to have penetrative sex with me when I was still too small to accommodate him. The pain was so bad I was convinced I was going to die. His horrible fat thing was so big I thought it was going to split me in two as he tried to force it between my legs. I imagined my whole body would tear in half and I would dissolve into nothingness. He was huge, drunk and awful at moments like that. He smelled vile, this great heavy man lying on top of me, trying to jab his way into me, not caring if I screamed and cried from the pain.

'Just relax,' he said, taking no notice of my sobbing. 'Stop making such a bloody fuss and it'll be over a lot quicker and it won't hurt so much.'

Each new picture would trigger a dozen other memories that would turn my stomach and fuel my anger and misery.

There are many things that can trigger childhood memories that have been suppressed for years. The moment that your own children reach the age that you were when you were abused is a typical one. Suddenly you look at them and imagine what was happening to you when you were that age, and you can't help picturing it happening to them, which unleashes a terrible flood of thoughts and makes you actually want to kill the person who abused you in the first place. Or a trauma like a divorce or the death of a parent can rock you so badly it releases all sorts of fears that were previously lodged out of sight in dark mental crevices. My relationship with Rodney must have acted like a drug, masking the real problems that lay underneath and which were the reasons why I had rushed so quickly and unwisely into the marriage in the first place. The moment the drug was withdrawn I was back where I had been as a confused and angry eighteen-year-old, facing the whole horrible truth about my past.

Although I felt terribly guilty about taking Brendan and Thomas away from Rodney and from their step-brothers and stepsister, they were remarkably cool about the whole thing. They were both accepting, happy to be back in Norwich and back at school with their friends on a regular basis. They were handling it all a hundred times better than I was and I was proud of them for that.

Living in a flat without a garden didn't feel like a home for any of us, especially after all the space we'd had out at the garden centre where the kids could run around wherever they wanted, and the brilliant house we had lived in before that. Even without the memories of my father haunting it, it wasn't a nice block to live in and we all felt hemmed in and claustrophobic. Opening a bottle of wine in the evening always helped to take the edge off it for me, but it was hardly a solution.

Although I was drinking heavily and taking drugs, I always tried to protect the boys from my habits. I remembered all too clearly how much Terry and I had hated it when Dad was drunk, and many of the terrible things he would do to us were done at those times. I made it a rule that I rarely drank during the day, unless I was sure the boys were safely out of the way, so the worst of it would happen after they had gone to bed at night or when they were over at Rodney's for the weekend. I'd had to agree they could go and see him, despite my fears that he would try to kidnap them and thus force me to go back to him. He was Thomas's father, and he was the only father figure Brendan had ever known, so it would have been cruel to stop them from seeing him. Often, when I was overcome with self-pity, I would ask myself if they would be better off with Rodney full-time, and I wondered if I was being selfish by hanging on to them when I was such a terrible person and must therefore be a terrible mother too. I loved them so much that I told myself I wanted to give them the best possible chance in life, even if it meant I had to give them up. In my sane moments, when I was willing to listen to what John was saying, I knew I had been a good mother considering all the circumstances, but those windows of clarity were becoming less and less frequent as my depression grew.

The memories of the things that Dad had made me do grew stronger as time passed rather than weaker, becoming full-scale flashbacks and vivid nightmares that would wake me up screaming and sweating, unable to get back to sleep. I'd be back there in a car with some sleazy businessman, feet up on the dashboard, slipping my knickers off, and then there was the horrible moment when he rolled on top of me, squashing me. So many years of terror and self-disgust each time I had to climb into a stranger's car, so many close brushes with death: 'Always get the money up front,' was a golden rule and the night when one of my punters said he'd pay later I knew there was something wrong.

Even though we were parked in the middle of nowhere, I fumbled to get out of his car and escape. But the moment my fingers touched the door handle he pulled me back into the seat with all his strength and smacked me hard in the mouth. I knew then not to argue or fight any more, just to give in. I felt like I was being raped. I felt violated, cheated and furious. Once he'd finished, he nicked whatever money I had in my purse before pushing me out of the car, flinging my bag out after me and driving off leaving me in a heap on the side of the road, scrabbling around on the ground for my scattered possessions, every last scrap of human dignity gone.

Memories like that were crowded into my head, fuelling my rage and my confusion. I felt incredibly angry about everything that had happened to me and I even started self-harming again, slashing at my wrists with anything that I could find. I had done it before, when I was a child. In all my confusion and anger and unhappiness I just wanted to hurt myself because I thought I was so worthless that I didn't deserve to be treated any better. Most of the anger that I had boiling away inside me during my teens was directed towards myself. I was often slashing my wrists or other parts of my body in self-disgust, taking overdoses or sitting in a bath tub trying to scrape myself clean with neat bleach and a scrubbing brush, not bothered that I was rubbing so hard I was drawing blood. It was as if I wanted to punish myself for being such a terrible person and those same feelings were back now, threatening to overwhelm me.

I was constantly thinking about killing myself, unable to see any other way out of the misery. I thought John would be better off without me, as would the boys, and I certainly didn't think either of my parents would care whether I was around or not. Dad would merely see it as confirmation that he had been right about me being useless all along and Mum would simply blame Dad.

I didn't know which way to turn or who to turn to. I didn't want to go back to Rodney but I felt guilty for being with John and every time he told me he loved me I would fly into a rage, which made me feel guilty all over again, and frightened that I would eventually drive him away and would be left completely alone. I'm ashamed to say that in my rages I would even lash out at him physically sometimes, usually when the last vestiges of my self-control had been drowned out by alcohol. After nights of violence and hysteria I would wake up hungover and with an ever-growing burden of guilt as I remembered my shameful behaviour of the night before. One moment I would be banishing John from my life and the next I would be hauling him back in. His patience with me was incredible. The fact that his wife was about to give him a child when I no longer could because of my sterilisation added to my insecurities and confusion.

One night, when everything seemed at its blackest, I decided I couldn't go on a moment longer and I tried to hang myself in the flat. I was drunk, angry, confused and desperate. John was about half an hour away and I was in the sitting room on the phone to him, having already made the necessary preparations. I had tied two dressing-gown cords together and fed the end over a beam in the loft. I had fetched myself a chair to stand on, which I intended to kick away from under me once I had the noose tied tightly round my neck.

'I'm going to hang myself,' I told John over the phone, convinced that he wouldn't be able to get back in time to save me.

He tried desperately to dissuade me, going on and on until in the end I lied and promised that I wouldn't, just to shut him up. I guess he must have been able to tell from my voice as I hung up the phone that I wasn't telling the truth because he leapt straight onto his motorbike and came roaring back to Norwich at full speed. Unable to get in through the front door because I had double-locked it, he climbed a drainpipe to the first-floor flat, scrambled in through a window and found me balanced on a chair trying to tie the noose round my neck. It wasn't hard for him to overpower me and lift me down. Instead of being grateful to him for coming to my rescue yet again, as I should have been, I was furious with him for stopping me when I had finally plucked up the courage to end it all. It felt as though I had failed yet again.

My friend Jane, who had been so supportive all the way through, was at her wits' end as to what to do with me. We had first met at school and both of us had been to Bramerton Lodge, a home for troubled children, so there wasn't much she didn't know about my past. She had actually met her partner in Bramerton (a man she is still with today), and she was pregnant with her second child at the same time as I was pregnant with Brendan.

Jane knew that one of the people who'd had the most influence on me in the past was the matron at Bramerton,

Rachel McQuarrie. Rachel and her husband had been instrumental in keeping me out of prison when I had got into a fight with another girl at the home and ended up slashing her hand with a piece of broken glass. They had even given up their Christmas one year in order to keep me company when I had no family of my own to go back to. Rachel had been at my side when I lost my first baby in a miscarriage, she had been one of my first visitors in the hospital after Brendan was born, and she had always treated me like a friend, even when I was behaving like a total idiot.

So when Jane realised I was in trouble again, she looked up Rachel McQuarrie's number in the phone book and gave her a call.

'I've rung Mrs Mac,' she told me, 'and she's agreed to meet you for coffee in the city tomorrow.'

It was an incredibly brave and wise thing for her to do, and very kind of Mrs Mac to spare me the time; after all, I hadn't been her responsibility for nearly ten years by then. I thought it would be nice to catch up with someone who had been such an important influence on my life. I don't know what Jane was expecting her to say to me, but I think she was as shocked as I was by what happened next.

Chapter Eleven

Finding Marion

It started out like any meeting between old friends as we settled down with our coffees and chatted about what had been going on in our lives since we last met, but conversation soon turned to the things that were now going on in my life and everything that I was going through. Mrs Mac had always been very easy for me to confide in and I probably told her more than I had even told Jane. It just came pouring out, the way it used to in the days at Bramerton when she allowed me to sit in her office during the day rather than going to lessons, finding little jobs for me to do and making me feel as though I wasn't a completely useless person. I think an ability to make people feel like that is one of the greatest gifts anyone can attain.

When I had finally run dry and fell silent, sitting there feeling a little self-conscious about the way I had taken over the conversation, Mrs Mac was quiet for a moment, looking at me thoughtfully before speaking.

'You need sorting out, Ria,' she said eventually, in the no-nonsense manner that had made her so successful in her career as the matron of a care home. 'You've hidden your past deep inside your head for years and it's eating away at you like a cancer. If you don't deal with it, it'll destroy you. If you aren't going to sort it out now you might as well go straight home and swallow another bottle of pills.'

I was shocked by the harshness of her words and I doubt I would have accepted them from anyone else. I had often picked fights in pubs over less. But Mrs Mac had earned my respect through years of showing that she cared and had my best interests at heart and I was willing to take seriously any advice she might give me, even if I initially found her words offensive. I opened my mouth to answer back but thought better and closed it again.

'You need to talk to a professional,' she went on, giving me the name of a counsellor who she thought would do me good, and then making the introductory call herself before I had a chance to protest.

Half an hour later I was sitting in an office a few doors away, with a woman I had never met before called Marion. It seemed that Mrs Mac was on the committee of a charity that Marion ran called Adult Survivors of Incest and Sexual Abuse, and believed that she would be the best person for me to talk to.

Yet again I felt angry, believing I had been conned and manipulated. The same stubborn streak that wouldn't allow me to accept that my doctor knew best when he suggested I should take anti-depressants was making me want to rebel now. If it hadn't been Mrs Mac who had insisted I probably would never have gone there at all. Even though I had agreed to do as she suggested, I was still cross. I had thought I was going out for a coffee and a friendly chat and here I was back in the system – at least that was how it felt. Part of me wanted to shout at my so-called friends for betraying me, but the other part knew that I needed help, that Mrs Mac was the most likely person to tell me the right thing to do and that it might at least be worth listening to what this woman had to say. I knew that however much I might resent it, I needed help desperately so I agreed that I would come and talk to Marion once a week, on Thursdays at 11 a.m.

I actually liked Marion the moment I met her. She looked slightly older than me, with the kindest smiling blue eyes. We had an immediate affinity and it wasn't long into the first meeting that I realised she was the most amazing person I had ever met. I'd had a week to calm down and think about things after my dressing down from Mrs Mac, and I knew that my old friend and supporter had been right yet again to steer me towards her. Marion wasn't like any of the social workers or care staff I had come across before. She had dedicated her whole life to helping victims of childhood sexual abuse and was a totally beautiful person. For the first time I knew I was talking to someone who truly did know how it felt to be in my position. Nothing I did or said surprised her. She had seen it all before and knew it was all perfectly normal for someone with my history. So many social workers had told me they understood over the years, but I never believed that they truly did – not like this.

I found that I could talk to Marion about anything, but I also found that the more I talked about the past the angrier I became with the whole world, starting with Mum and Dad and all the relatives who I felt had let us down through the years of our childhood. I was also angry with Rodney for refusing to understand why I felt the way I did and for continuing the abuse in his own way. I was letting all my anger and resentment come to the surface and it was a painful process, forcing me to think about all the things that I had been trying so hard not to think about, but which I had merely been hording inside my head until they fought free on their own in the form of flashbacks and nightmares.

'The past is the past,' was all Rodney had kept saying whenever I brought up the subject of my childhood. 'Why do you want to put yourself through all this again? Why don't you just come back to me and get on with your life and your family? It could all be so simple.'

There was a logical part of my brain that could see what he meant. How nice it would be if I could do that – wipe the slate clean and just start all over again. But it was like trying to build a house on sand. Whenever I had tried in the past it would seem as if I was getting somewhere for a while and then the sands would shift and the whole structure would collapse once more. I needed to find a way to give myself a solid foundation to build my future on.

Rodney was still doing everything he could to persuade me to go back to him, using the boys to help him put the pressure on whenever the opportunity arose. As I had feared, some weekends he held onto them when he should have been bringing them back and I ended up having to ask the police yet again to come with me to retrieve them, or I would have to go to court to get an order. The last thing I wanted to do was make it difficult for him to see them, and he knew that and worked it to his advantage.

Despite my sessions with Marion the stress continued to be enormous. Although I was becoming deeply depressed I was still refusing to take anti-depressants. I preferred to deal with the bad feelings my own way, which meant drinking heavily, which I can now see never helped anyone. Marion and the doctor explained that I was suffering from something called post-traumatic stress disorder and that talking to Marion was bringing everything to the surface, like lancing a boil. I was having the most terrible nightmares, which Marion was encouraging me to write down as soon as I woke up each morning, while I could still remember them, so we could talk about them at our next session.

In a recurrent nightmare, I was running through a big house looking for the boys. I could hear them but I couldn't get to them. I'd turn down a new passage and there would be a group of winos sneering at me or even being sick on me and I couldn't get away. Each passage I chose turned out to be the wrong one. Afterwards I would wake up anxious and exhausted.

One of the things that frequently preyed on my mind was that I kept hearing how people who were abused as children often grew up to be abusers themselves. Dad always claimed that he was the way he was because of what had happened to him as a child. Personally I didn't think there was any excuse for doing what he did, and in fact if you had suffered like that yourself you should be all the more aware of why it was wrong to inflict the same pain on someone else. But so many people told me that abused children became abusers I became terrified that I was going to follow the same path and would be unable to stop myself. I was discovering that many of the emotions I was going through were standard responses to having been abused, so did that mean I was programmed to abuse my own children as well?

Once I started thinking like that, I realised I didn't really know the appropriate ways to behave with the boys as they grew up, because Dad had never taught me. When did it stop being appropriate for me to walk about the house naked in front of them? When should I stop bathing them? When should I stop cuddling them? The more I worried about it, the less I was able to see anything clearly. I became scared of what might be lurking undetected in my subconscious. It made me angry to think that Dad's selfish actions could end up affecting my relationship with my boys and I spilled all my fears out to Marion.

'Have you ever wanted to abuse them?' she asked, matter-of-factly.

'No,' I replied, indignantly, 'of course not.'

'Well then, you don't need to worry about it,' she said, as if that was the end of the matter. 'You will do the right things automatically.'

It was hugely reassuring but still it didn't set my fears entirely to rest.

On Guy Fawkes night that year the boys were staying over with Rodney and I had been out drinking with John, as I usually did when they were away. For some reason my anger, which was never far beneath the surface, boiled up to the highest pitch it had ever reached by the time we got home. I can't remember why, but Mum was round at the flat when we got back there and that might have been one factor that caused the explosion. I hated that flat so much that just walking into it could tip me over the edge sometimes, making me want to destroy everything in it. Whatever the reason, I completely lost the plot. I was thrashing out all over the place and I started hitting John, screaming at him to get out and leave me alone.

As always he was incredibly understanding and refused to leave, so I smashed the kitchen up in my frustration, trying in vain to wipe away all the memories that every room and every possession held for me. I was hurling plates and glasses against the walls, sweeping surfaces clean onto the floor, and I finally punched my fist through the window. The release of tension in the crash of broken glass felt satisfying, so I did it again. The only other time I had done this much damage was when I faked a meltdown in a care home when I was a kid, to try to get the same attention I'd seen one of the other wild kids getting. But this time I wasn't faking it; I had actually lost control and no longer knew what I was doing or why.

John realised there was nothing he could do and phoned Marion for help. Luckily for him it was a Friday night, when she always worked late. He explained quickly what was going on, although she could probably hear me raging and smashing away in the background anyway.

'Speak to Marion,' he pleaded, holding out the phone to me.

'No, fuck off!' I screamed, continuing on my rampage around the flat, on a mission to break the few things that were left. I didn't want to speak to her because I didn't want to stop feeling angry. It actually felt good and deep inside I knew it would feel bad as soon as I stopped and thought about what I was doing. I wanted more good feelings, more cleansing destruction before I had to pay the inevitable price of guilt and embarrassment. Seeing all the broken glass and crockery and carnage around me felt like a sort of release and I began to calm down as I ran out of things to destroy.

Eventually I came to a halt and snatched the phone from John, panting from the exertion, ready to shout at Marion if she annoyed me. But as soon as I heard her voice I felt foolish and guilty for being so childish and selfish and for doing so much damage.

'This is good,' Marion said warmly. 'A breakthrough.'

'A breakthrough?' I couldn't help laughing at her words as I gazed around at the wrecked flat. 'In what way?'

'Because you are venting your anger outwardly, taking it out on the world around you instead of taking it out on yourself by self-harming or taking an overdose. All the things you have broken tonight can be repaired or replaced; they're not important. You are what is important.'

'Yeah?' I was trying to take in her words through my drunkenness and to understand what she was saying.

'You have a lot to be angry about, Ria,' she went on. 'You have every right to be. A lot of people have let you down in your life. All those years of suppressing it have taken their toll but now the volcano has finally erupted, which is good.'

Not only had she managed to make me laugh in the midst of my rage, but she had actually made me feel less guilty about destroying my own home. It felt as though the explosion was a natural part of whatever internal journey it was Marion had been guiding me through, something that anyone in my position with my past might experience. In some ways it was as if she had been deliberately leading me to this point, pushing me to let it all out and face up to my demons rather than trying to ignore them. I'm sure there must be millions of people who have been through the sort of experiences I have been through, who have not had the luck to meet someone like Marion and so have never been shown how to deal with their anger, so I count myself as deeply fortunate.

Marion became my lifeline through all those months of pain and despair as I worked through my problems, and my weekly sessions with her were the only things that gave me hope. Slowly but surely she was healing me. One of the huge changes was that for the first time in my life I stopped loving my father. Up until then, part of me still wanted him to look after me and put things right, and it was hard to let that go. I was finally able to see clearly what he had done to me and I no longer believed I was to blame for everything that had gone wrong just because he said I was. I couldn't forgive him, but that didn't matter. I just needed to know that none of it was my fault.

Marion's main preoccupation in our sessions was dealing with how I thought and felt about myself, because at that time I believed I was nobody. I was Rodney's ex-wife, Brendan and Thomas's mum and Dad's daughter, but I had no idea who I actually was or what I wanted from life. I felt that Marion was the only person in the world who understood me and could help me.

She recommended a book called *The Courage to Heal* by Ellen Bass and Laura Davies, which was to become my bible. I hadn't read a book since I was about fourteen but this one hooked me immediately because it seemed to be talking directly to me. I bought two copies, one of which I kept beside my bed and the other I would carry with me everywhere I went. By reading about the experiences of other women I realised that Marion was right and all the feelings I was experiencing were normal. Sometimes I would read the same sentence over and over again, underlining it to reassure myself that the things I had always thought were wrong with me were a normal reaction to the childhood I had been forced to endure. I even began to believe that if I worked through every chapter of the book I would end up being 'cured'. For a while, I became as addicted and dependent on the book as I had previously been on drink and drugs and self-destruction.

In my eagerness to become well I tried to rush things and got annoyed and frustrated with myself whenever I had another setback. It would be many years before I learned how to be patient with myself, before I realised that I could not change life-long habits of thinking and feeling overnight. But at last I was on the right road.

Chapter Twelve

The Inner Child

Marion talked a lot to me about my 'inner child' and although I trusted her completely I was still uncomfortable discussing such things. It made me feel self-conscious and I would try to avoid the issue or I would poo-poo it as ridiculous when all the time a tiny voice at the back of my mind was telling me that she might have a point. I began to sense that she was becoming impatient with me. One day as I was leaving she spoke out.

'You need to think about where we are going with this counselling, Ria,' she said, stopping me in my tracks. 'We have talked and talked about everything that has happened to you, but you have still not really "felt" it. If ever I touch on something that might make you cry, you instantly change the subject. You talk about your abuse as if it were a shopping list, cataloguing it rather than feeling it.'

Her words made me angry but I knew that what she said was true because both my father and Rodney had taught me that it was useless to cry, that I would be mocked for it as well, and that it could even lead to me receiving another beating. I had prided myself on becoming a tough old gypsy wife; I didn't 'do' crying.

Marion wanted to take things a step deeper and I knew I had to trust her, but I was scared of what might happen if I let myself go, of what might come pouring out. At the same time I didn't want to risk losing Marion because I didn't feel ready to cope without her. Over the following few sessions she tried all ways to get through to me, and then one day she tried something new.

'What would Ria look like if she was seven years old and standing here in the office now?' she asked. 'Describe her for me.'

Taken unawares I conjured up a mental picture of myself at seven and began to describe the little blonde girl I saw in front of me.

'She is standing there now,' I said, 'with her head down, too embarrassed to speak up for herself, not making eye contact. She is pretty but obviously terrified, battered and bruised, lonely and scared.'

I was shocked by the vividness of the picture I could see of this abused and frightened child. She looked so sweet and vulnerable and innocent, nothing like the horrible, unattractive creature that my father had always told me I was. She looked as though she had been abandoned and rejected by everyone.

I remembered the way she had to find food for herself and her brother, maybe jam sandwiches if there was any bread, or chips made from potatoes she dug up in the garden. I remembered the way she had to do all the washing and ironing and get herself ready for school. Then I thought about a summer holiday with a local family called the Bunns, who were very kind. When the little seven-year-old girl got sunburn, Ann Bunn gently rubbed on calamine lotion and it was a revelation that grown-ups could do caring things like that because she wasn't used to anyone doing anything for her at all.

It broke my heart to think of how much that little girl had been forced to go through and I was shocked to think of all the things I had done over the years to put her in situations where she continued to be abused by the people she loved, by complete strangers and even by herself. It was a revelation because I had never allowed myself to see her like that before and this time I was unable to stop the tears from flowing. In fact I didn't even try.

Once the sluice gates had been opened everything poured out and when I got home I broke down and sobbed uncontrollably for days, unable to get out of bed, just lying there, listening to Richard Clayderman playing sad songs, as if I was deliberately trying to exorcise the sadness from my soul once and for all, forcing it all to pour out.

The tears were painful but at the same time strangely cleansing and healing. I had finally embarked on the last leg of my journey of discovery and had found the inner child that Marion had been telling me about for so long. I felt so sad about everything that had happened to little Ria and the feeling lasted for weeks, leaving me immobilised and unable to face anything in life. It was hard but even as it was happening I understood that I had to go through it if I wanted to come out the other side.

'Just because you have found your inner child doesn't mean things are going to change overnight,' Marion warned me next time I went to see her. 'You still have a lot to learn and to forgive yourself for.'

She was right, of course, as always, but it was still a turning point and from that moment things started, very slowly, to get better.

'What are you doing for the rest of the day?' she asked at the end of one session.

'I'm going to the beach,' I said, surprised to hear my own words, which seemed to be coming from a little girl inside me, 'And I'm going to paddle in the waves.'

We both laughed at the idea and agreed that it would be a good idea to do what the little girl inside was suggesting. The boys didn't need collecting from school for a good few hours, so I could forget about being a grown-up for a while and just do something to please myself. As I walked to my car it felt as if I now had the little girl with me, walking beside me. I had unlocked her from the prison I had been keeping her in for years. For the first time in my life I felt I was doing something for myself, listening to myself, and it was an amazing experience.

Just arriving at a beach can help to put your troubles into perspective. The immensity and emptiness of the ocean stretching away to the horizon, the power of the waves on the shore, the fact that everyone is sitting or wandering aimlessly, apparently enjoying themselves and escaping from the everyday worries of their lives: it all reminds you of how small you are and how irrelevant your problems are in the great scheme of the world, puny compared to the might of nature and time. A little matter like incest means nothing compared to the size of an ocean.

I kicked off my shoes and walked across the soft, damp sand, away from everything, squinting out into the glare of the sky reflected on the water. The cold salty waves startled me as they washed over my bare legs and feet, but within a few seconds I had adapted to the change of temperature and the water began to feel warm and soothing. As I paddled and played the waves splashed further up my legs and I giggled with childish shock and delight. I lifted my cotton dress as high as I dared, but the waves still caught the hem, exciting me and making me feel naughty. It was as if I was witnessing the wonder of the ocean for the first time as I twirled and jumped, revelling in the warm sun and the cool breeze and the glory of a wonderful day, spreading my arms wide, skipping and dancing as the tears trickled down my face and dried in the warm breeze. I didn't care who might be watching or what they might be thinking.

It felt as though I had been set free, released from the handcuffs of depression for the first time ever. The iron door of my mental prison cell had blocked my view of the world, preventing me from seeing the beautiful universe full of joy and laughter that existed outside. Behind my door I had been able to see only heartache and pain and sordid pictures of a world that was full of danger and of people who wanted to hurt me. I had been scared and lonely in that cell, but safe and secure at the same time. I imagined that the waves were washing away all the filth, guilt and disgust. I realised that I was worth something after all, that I had suffered enough and now it was time to build a new life and I knew that the ocean would always be there for me to return to when I felt I needed to remind myself of this feeling.

I headed back to the car with the tears still flowing, bathed in an inner glow of happiness and peace, and set off to pick the boys up from school. For the first time in my life I felt hopeful and strong and proud. I knew now that life was for living, not just for surviving.

At the height of that euphoria I believed all my troubles were over, but of course they weren't. I had, however, been given a glimpse of how good life can be. I now knew for the first time what true happiness felt like, the feeling I had been chasing every time I poured myself a drink or swallowed a tablet but had never been able to grasp. Now, if only I could find a way of holding onto it, my journey would be over.

I knew the key to capturing this strength and happiness lay in my Thursday morning sessions with Marion. Week on week, I found myself understanding more, learning more and becoming more powerful. Some weeks could be very distressing, and I was still crippled by depression that stopped me getting out of bed some days, but even at the worst moments I looked forward to seeing her because I knew that whatever happened, it would take me forwards a bit more.

Writing down my nightmares for Marion had become another form of release and I found I actually enjoyed the process of putting my thoughts down on paper. I started to write more about how I felt and about some of the things that had happened to me in the past. It was like another form of therapy. Marion seemed to know exactly the right and kind thing to say or do at any given moment. One day I went in and she had bought me a present. It was a little jewellery box with a key. When you wound it up and lifted the lid a tiny ballerina would unfold and dance to the music it played. It was something I had always wanted but had never had, and I was delighted. I had believed that I went without those sorts of gifts as a little girl because nobody cared enough, but with one gesture Marion proved it was never too late to heal those wounds.

Talking to Marion had also opened me up to new ideas, helping me to consider what other people were saying to me. I suppose she was gradually making me more trusting of my fellow man. She made me willing to listen to what the doctors had to say to me, whereas in the past I had always thought I knew best – still the same stroppy teenager I had been in the care homes, the one who never wanted to accept the authority of her elders. I was still seeing the doctor about my depression, still feeling worried that it wasn't right to be spending so much of my time just lying around in bed, so when he prescribed me Prozac I decided to give it a go, to open my mind to something new. What did I have to lose?

Chapter Thirteen

Chasing Happy Ever After

I had only been taking the Prozac for two weeks before I changed my mind about it. I decided that if lying in bed and feeling sad was what my body and brain wanted to do at this stage of my healing process, then it was probably the best way forward, a natural way of mending. I didn't want to risk becoming dependent on drugs, even legal ones, so I decided to go back to trusting nature. I realised that taking speed was giving me as many downs as it was highs, and so I stopped taking that too. I guess I can't have been addicted to it if I was able to stop at will. I had always been lucky not to become addicted to the drugs that I had taken in the past, or to drink, but I knew that there was always a risk that one day I would push my luck too far. Marion was making me feel confident that I would eventually come out the other side of the depression if I could just bear to allow it to take its course without putting any mood-altering chemicals in my body.

John remained incredibly supportive and strong throughout the whole process. He was proving to be a bit of saint really, considering what he had to put up with from me. It was a role that he seemed to relish playing – not that there weren't good times in our relationship as well as bad.

The good thing about being officially a depressive was that the council agreed to re-house me and the boys, since the cramped condition of the flat was obviously a big contributing factor to the illness. Once I had a house with a bit more space John moved in permanently and things began to improve for us all. It was as if a little light had been allowed to shine into the darker recesses of my moods.

As I spent more time thinking about how I was going to find a way to be happy, I started to ask a lot of questions about the existence of God, a subject I had never given much thought to in the past. I wanted to find something I could cling to in my anger and bewilderment and I knew that a lot of people found comfort in religion, so maybe I could too. Talking with Marion had made me much more open-minded and much more willing to consider other ways of looking at life. Marion didn't bring the subject up until I did and then she told me she was a Christian herself. She said that she believed there was no way she would have been able to do the work she did without God's help. Since I was already deeply impressed with her achievements I was more than willing to try to discover what the secret of her success was and started to ask her questions. It was only then that I discovered her surname was Godwin, and to my mind the 'God-' prefix seemed like a bit of sign.

I also found out that John's parents were religious too, attending church every Sunday and getting heavily involved in their local community, which gave me some-one else to talk to and question. They had thought it best that they didn't meet me for the first year of our relation-ship, out of respect for John's wife. I could understand that since they had no way of knowing if John and I were going to last as a couple and they needed to concentrate on the arrival of their grandchild. When we were still together at the end of the year, however, they invited me to their home and were totally friendly, supportive and kind.

They led a very idyllic life, complete with a thatched cottage in the countryside. John's little sister, who was the same age as Brendan, used to have piano lessons and ballet lessons and all the wonderful little-girl things that I had never had and never thought I was worthy of, although I had always secretly longed for them. I watched her Dad brushing her hair one day and that simple, loving and caring action hit a chord deep inside me. It wasn't that I was jealous because I was happy for her to be so loved and looked after, but it reminded me of the unkindness and emptiness of my own relationship with my father. He would never have done something so simple and gentle for me without having an ulterior motive, without wanting something for himself. I remembered how he used to take sadistic pleasure in washing my hair in the bath with freezing cold water, just to hear me scream, and how he would then tug roughly at the knots with a brush as if it was a punishment. Watching John's father being so gentle and loving reminded me of my friend telling me about how her husband washed her hair for her as a gesture of love. I told Marion about how seeing that simple act had affected me when I saw her the following week.

'Well,' she said, 'next time you come in I'll brush your hair for you.'

We never actually got round to that but it felt nice to know that she would be willing to do it for me. These tiny gestures between human beings are the things that make us feel that we are worth something, that we are loved.

Once my eyes had suddenly been opened to the idea of religion and God, I started to notice the church that we lived close to, which I used to want to go to as a child. It was called St Catherine's and was one of only two churches in Norwich to have bells. Whenever I had mentioned it to Dad as a child he would always scoff and put me off. I was going to be in the school nativity play there one year, but he forbade it. I guess he thought it might allow me the opportunity to fall too far under the influence of other people, people who might undermine his complete authority over me. He would never let me go to Sunday school either, or to sing in school choirs or even attend the school services that were held in the church. He managed to convince me that I wasn't good enough for such things; that churches weren't meant for people as useless and ugly and wicked as me. Not content with abusing me physically, mentally and emotionally, he wanted to destroy any possible spiritual life I might have had as well. He hated anything outside his control, which might allow me to talk to people who would have very different attitudes towards life from his own.

So I had given up thinking about it and over the years St Catherine's church had become merely a background feature in my life, just like any other building in Norwich, a city that has a church for every week of the year (and a pub for every day of the year). When they are so commonplace, it's easy to walk past these buildings every day, lost in your own thoughts and worries, not even noticing what is staring you in the face. Now that I had started to think about God, I became angry with Him too. If He existed and He was all-seeing and all-powerful, how could He have allowed all the things that had been done to me as a little girl? I knew from talking to Marion that I was far from alone in the suffering I had gone through as an innocent and helpless child; so why did He allow it to happen to so many of the children of the world? That naturally led to me wondering about all the other atrocities and tragedies that I read about in the papers and heard about on the news every day. Why did He permit so much suffering amongst innocent people? All my thoughts and feelings were raw, as though my soul had been laid bare.

One day, when I was at a particularly low ebb, I took myself off for a walk and ended up sitting in the church-yard of St Catherine's, staring up at the amazing building that I had walked past so many times before and never really seen. I remembered having my first-ever cigarette in the grounds when I was eleven years old. Thinking back to the past started me crying again, something I seemed to be doing most of the time at that stage. I was wondering if the pain would ever end and questioning what would become of me in the future, when I became aware of a man's voice speaking to me.

'Are you okay?' he asked.

I looked up with a jump and came face to face with the curate. I had been so absorbed in my own thoughts I hadn't even heard him entering the churchyard or coming over to me.

'I'm fine,' I said, embarrassed and quickly wiping away the tears as I stood up to go home. I felt like a naughty schoolgirl who had been caught trespassing.

'Do you want to go inside the church?' he asked.

'It's the middle of the day,' I said, flustered. 'It's all locked up. I'll just go home.'

'This is your church too, you know,' he said. 'I'll unlock it for you and you can spend as much time in there as you want. You can talk to me if you like, or you can just spend some time in there on your own.'

I was too stunned to refuse the offer. I couldn't understand why he was being so kind to someone as worthless and undeserving as me. Did he have some sinister ulterior motive? Dad would immediately have assumed he had, but he seemed pretty safe to me so I followed him into the cool, silent interior of the building and told him I would like to be alone. He didn't seem the least bit offended. He just smiled and nodded, gestured for me to make myself at home and went about his business, leaving me alone in the quietness. I sat down in the front pew, gazed up at all the beautiful stained glass and the carvings and felt the tears rising up again. As I cried my heart out I felt a strange kind of peace settling over me, as if God was holding me close and comforting me, allowing me to let it all out. It felt I'd reached another turning point on my road to recovery, as if I was swapping my dad for God, as if He was now going to be my 'big daddy'. It seemed I was being offered another possible route to escape from the malevolent influences of my childhood. Despite all those years that my father had managed to keep me out of this place, in the end he had failed and God had succeeded in winning me over. 'Suffer the little children to come unto me and forbid them not': that's what Jesus says in the Bible.

I would love to be able to say that all my problems vanished that day once my sobbing had subsided and I was left feeling drained and peaceful, but it would be a long way from the truth. Just like those hours spent at the beach, sitting in that pew and quietly contemplating the beauty and tranquillity of the building around me had given me a glimpse of what might be possible if I continued on my road to recovery, but the feeling was snatched away from me again as soon as I returned to the real world with all its problems and memories and pains; two steps forward, one step back.

The curate had introduced himself as Richard, and he grew to be a close friend to me and to John over the coming years; someone who accepted us as we were and never judged us by anything we might have done in the past. It was a while before I was able fully to convince myself that I was worthy of God's love, just as it was taking time to shake off all the other beliefs that Dad had beaten into me during my formative years. With Richard's gentle encouragement I tried going to church services to worship with other people but I found it difficult. The services seemed old-fashioned and irrelevant to the realities of my life outside the walls of the church. I guess the timelessness of religious services is one of the attractions for some people, reminding them of the eternal truths, but I preferred to talk to God directly, one to one, through the poems and other writings that I was doing more and more of.

I suppose writing was another way of praying. I have come to believe that any form of spirituality is very personal and that everyone has to work out what is right for them. I loved churches as pieces of architecture and vessels of history, and as retreats from the noise and rush of the outside world, but at that stage I didn't like them when they were full of other people. I liked an empty church where I could feel at peace and safe from other people, just as I liked going for long, lonely walks, especially on the beach, where I could feel in touch with nature. I didn't feel any need to be christened (a task Mum and Dad never got round to for me although they did get Terry christened at the insistence of my grandmother), but I could see that many people felt better for it. I have come to realise that anything that makes you feel good about yourself and the world you live in has to be worth a try. I'd tried drink and drugs, I'd tried motherhood and marriage, and each of them had brought some respite from depression and despair and self-loathing, but it had always proved temporary and was never enough to rid myself completely of these inner demons. I was going to have to search harder and longer before I achieved that.

John and I had become a permanent couple, despite all Rodney's efforts to split us up and make life difficult for us. In the end he left us alone, just as he had eventually left Sue and Kevin alone. I still considered committing suicide from time to time, but the respites between these bouts of intense depression were gradually becoming longer as I found more ways of coping with them, making life easier. Suicide was a concept that I had been familiar with all my life. Even when I was small I used to hear Dad saying he was going to kill himself after Mum left because she was the love of his life and he didn't want to go on without her. I remembered the night he had terrified my brother and me by swallowing weedkiller and then staggering upstairs to die. We had no idea how serious he was in his intentions or whether he was just attention-seeking but we were so scared of losing him and being left with no parents at all that we called for a doctor to come and save him. He didn't have to go to hospital but no one ever troubled to explain to us what had happened, or to check that we were all right after such a traumatic experience. The point was that from the beginning of my life I had been aware of self-inflicted death being an option should the pain of existence become too intense and unbearable.

There were lots of wonderful times during my life with John. He still had his motorbike and I loved to ride pillion behind him, the rush of the wind and the freedom of the road bringing back memories of my early days with Brian, who was my first serious love and Brendan's father. John and I would go on camping weekends and holidays, sometimes with the boys, sometimes just the two of us. We also went out dancing together and did all the things that Rodney would never have dreamed of doing with me, things that made me feel as though he cared about me, liked to be with me, loved me. He made me feel that I was attractive and worth something in the world. These good times interspersed the difficult ones like bursts of sunshine between the storm clouds.

Nine months after I drove away from the mobile home at the garden centre, once the council had re-housed us and John had been able to move in properly, we started to lay plans for getting married as soon as possible after our divorces had come through. We both honestly believed that once we had done that we would be able to live happily ever after, finally putting all our troubles behind us. We were in love and I was sure that we would never split up. We had survived so much together and I had put him through such hell, but he had always been there for me and shown that he could be relied upon. John found a new job in Norwich, which was closer to home, and it looked as though we really were moving forward.

In my head I was building a fantasy of being at the centre of a big white wedding in my special church, surrounded by bridesmaids and the whole traditional scene. I set about laying plans for our special day, as if I was living in some sort of real-life fairy tale. In the past I would never have believed that such things could happen to someone as worthless as me, but John had made me feel so secure with him I could actually envisage us having a happy future together.

Since I was certain that I didn't want Dad to be there on my wedding day, ruining what I was planning would be the happiest day of my life by stirring up hideous old memories, John's father offered to give me away. It was such a kind gesture. He had heard enough of my story to know I wouldn't want Dad within a mile of the church that day but guessed I would also be sad not to have a father figure there for me. All the signs were good; it looked as though I just might be happy at last. John was also good with my mum, just as Rodney had been. It seemed it was easier to be her son-in-law than it had ever been to be one of her children.

John and I were finally married in November 1994. We couldn't actually hold the wedding in the church because we had both been married before, but we were allowed to have a 'blessing service', which was everything a normal wedding would have been but without the legal bits (we'd done them before at the registry office). I didn't suffer from any of the last-minute doubts that I had when I married Rodney. I know it's a cliché but I think as I stood at the altar in St Catherine's I really did feel like the happiest woman in the world.

Chapter Fourteen

More to Me Than Frying Eggs

We were all so happy as a family after the wedding, I felt very optimistic about our future together and even thought I probably didn't need my weekly sessions with Marion any more. Although I would have liked to go on seeing her forever just because I enjoyed her company so much, I was conscious that there must be hundreds of other people who would be able to benefit from having some of her time as much as I had and that I needed to share her. I realised I could never be completely healed from the trauma of my past but I believed she had given me the knowledge and the tools I needed to deal with anything that fate might now throw at me. I had a nice house, a supportive husband, happy kids, and I'd got a job working at a health and fitness club called the Sports Village, where I eventually ended up being a catering supervisor. It seemed I had finally been cured of my past.

Marion agreed that I didn't need to see her any more. 'But we are friends now,' she assured me, 'so you can always phone or meet me for a cup of coffee if you ever get stuck.'

John got on well with Brendan and Thomas and respected their relationship with Rodney completely, never feeling threatened by the fact that Rodney saw them regularly and was their 'dad'. Rodney didn't bother to hide the fact that he wasn't happy about me moving on, but he pretty much left me to it. He still got on well with Mum and told her that it didn't matter who I married because he still knew I would go back to him one day. I guess he said the same things about Sue when she first got together with Kevin. I could understand now why she had been so relieved when I came along and took the pressure off her. Although I tried to be on reasonably friendly terms with Rodney for the sake of the boys, I didn't like the idea that he still saw me as his property, just out to John on loan as it were.

'I'll wait ten years for her if necessary,' he told Mum.

In a way I suppose it was flattering, but it also felt a bit spooky, as if he believed he had some sort of control over me and the course of my future. I was still completely determined that I was never going to go back to a life like the one I'd led with him for eight years, no matter what he might believe.

Around this time, I heard some terrible news about another ex of mine. Brian had had a horrible accident in which he fell from a balcony when drunk and suffered head injuries and brain damage. I went to visit him in the convalescent home where he was being cared for and, while he looked the same as ever, his memory had completely gone and he obviously didn't know who I was. I tried to chat about the past and told him how his son Brendan was getting on, but he forgot what I had said minutes later. A few months later, I saw him selling copies of *The Big Issue* in Norwich town centre, but I didn't go over to say hello that time. He wouldn't have known me.

My main preoccupation had become trying to work out what I wanted to do with my life now that the boys were getting older and didn't need to have me at home all day. I had always worked whenever Rodney would allow it and since leaving him, I had flitted between catering and bar jobs before settling at the Sports Village, but I was beginning to feel that I wanted to do something that would make a difference in the world. When I was eighteen my social worker, Doris, had told me that she believed I was capable of going to college but at the time there was no way I had the confidence to follow it up, and Rodney would never have allowed it anyway.

'You could study to be whatever you wanted to be,' she had said and her words had stuck in my memory, giving me something to cling to from time to time when I felt I was drowning in low self-esteem.

The problem, however, was that I had never had any idea what I wanted to be. I still didn't have the necessary confidence to believe that I could do anything useful in the world. From the moment I met Rodney I just wanted to have a family and live the life that I had missed out on in my childhood. Now I realised that wasn't going to be enough. I wasn't even thirty years old by then and still had my entire adult life ahead of me. I wanted to do something useful with it as Marion and Mrs Mac did, rather than fritter it away and build up a bank of regrets about the past like Mum and Dad.

Whatever I decided to do, I knew I was going to have to start back at the bottom of the ladder because my education had ground to a halt when I was about fourteen. I hadn't really read anything more than a magazine or newspaper since then, apart from the self-help books Marion had introduced me to. I was eager to change all that, but not sure how to go about it. I wondered if perhaps I should become a social worker, helping kids who had been through similar traumas to me, like the people I had come across working in the various homes I had been to, or like Doris. But when I looked into it I discovered you needed the equivalent of five GCSEs and I had none. I could do a full-time, two year Access Course, but I didn't think I could fit that in with my responsibilities for the boys while continuing to work in order to bring in money.

I decided to start gradually by doing one GCSE a year, since I had plenty of time, and I enrolled on an adult education GCSE course in sociology. I hadn't done any sort of studying for years and the first day I turned up at our local community centre I almost ran straight home again in a panic, terrified of having my ignorance exposed, of being asked a question I couldn't answer, and of being humiliated and shown up in front of the others. Hauling every last ounce of courage to the surface, I forced myself to stay in the classroom while everyone settled down. People started to introduce themselves and I soon realised that everyone was going to be on my side, wanting to help me, wanting me to succeed, and that we were all in the same position. It was an incredibly supportive bunch of people who kept me going through the early stages as I found my feet and found that I loved studying even though I found it incredibly hard.

Realising I needed extra help if I wasn't going to fall behind the others, I signed up for a six-week course to work on my basic literary skills. One of the first tasks on the course was to write down ten things we felt we were good at. I sat staring at the paper, sucking my pen and shuffling my feet, not able to think of a single thing to say. Looking around the room I could see that everyone else was scribbling away, but my head was completely empty. There wasn't anything I had ever done that I hadn't been told I was useless at, no ambition I had ever harboured that someone hadn't told me I should forget because I would never succeed. In the end the only skill I could think of was that I was good at frying eggs because it was an art I had mastered through working in cafés and producing endless cooked breakfasts for customers or back at home for friends and family. That was it – nearly thirty years old and the only thing I thought I was good at was frying an egg!

I stared at the paper, not wanting to look up in case I caught someone's eye, just wanting to run home, climb back into bed and cry. The whole studying thing suddenly seemed like a complete waste of time, a foolish delusion. Inside my head I could almost hear Dad and Rodney sniggering at my stupidity. But no one in the classroom laughed at me for only being able to fry eggs; they just started to show me, gently and persuasively, that I was mistaken, that I was actually good at a lot of different things. My confidence began to inch forward, growing as slowly and invisibly as a tree in early spring, the changes only visible when I looked back in weeks to come at the low point I had started from.

While I was climbing up out of my depression and away from my insecurities, however, something was happening inside John's head. All the time that I had been an emotional wreck he had been my rock and my saviour, the one who made everything better, the strong one. Along with Marion he had been the main reason why I had been able to get as far as I had, but as I started to get my life together and actually became happy, something strange happened: we seemed to exchange roles, as if I was sucking all the strength and purpose from his life into my own. He started to become reclusive, withdrawn and depressed, and my newly discovered vigour for life seemed to make him feel insecure. It was hard to understand because I would have been the first to admit that in the early days of our relationship I had given him plenty of cause to feel insecure with all my shouting and ranting and my pessimistic predictions. But throughout all of that he had remained stoic and patient, always there for me, never wavering. I had assumed that once we were married we would be able to 'live happily ever after', just as he had always said we would. But now we had actually reached the point where that might be possible it seemed he was seeing things differently.

'Now we're married,' he told me, 'I have nothing else to offer you.'

It was as if he felt that by fulfilling his promise to save me from my demons and marry me he no longer had a purpose in life, had nothing else to give. He did have a stressful job as a 24-hour on-call mechanic at the time, which might have gone some of the way to explaining why his confidence and sense of purpose were crumbling, but it was still a puzzle. Maybe a lot of men feel like that about their partners and some react like Rodney, by trying to control the women in their lives, while others, like John, merely become despondent and feel inadequate. He gave up work soon after that, and then he stopped even going out of the house, just sitting around watching television all day. It was as if all his strength and purpose had drained away at the same time as mine had grown. It felt as though I had lost my knight in shining armour.

If I had been stronger and wiser myself, maybe I could have helped him to see that me becoming empowered was a good thing for both of us, but I was still only at the early stages of my development, only just able to keep myself on the straight and narrow. I didn't have the spare energy to support someone else who appeared to be going through some sort of nervous breakdown. He became increasingly insecure with every passing day, unable to get himself re-started, wanting to be with me all the time, like a small child. I wished he would go to counselling to help sort out everything I had put him through over the previous eighteen months, but he didn't, so maybe his crack-up was a reaction to everything that had happened before.

Whatever the reasons for the breakdown, we both failed miserably when it came to dealing with it. Instead of seeking professional help, we argued constantly. Our life together became a war zone, although it was all about shouting and crying and there was none of the violence I had been used to with Rodney and Dad. Despite the fact that I was moving forward in other areas of my life, I still wasn't ready to cope with anything like this. I couldn't be strong for him in the way he had been for me in the past, however much I might want to be. I felt that every complaint John came up with was a personal attack on me. He would bring up mistakes that I had made in the past, which I believed he had dealt with but which obviously still bothered him because he would go over and over and over them until I thought I was going to scream, and sometimes did. We just kept repeating the same behaviour and things got worse and worse between us. As always my way of dealing with problems was to run away and get drunk, which did nothing to help John's feelings of insecurity. We were trapped in a brand new vicious circle.

For three years we limped along in this miserable state, regularly splitting up and then getting back together again, just as I used to do with Rodney. I was desperate to rescue the situation and not to fail yet again. I couldn't understand why I couldn't get free of this cycle of behaviour, however much I might want to. We tried going to marriage guidance together every week for about eight months, but it didn't solve anything – in fact the rows just seemed to get worse. Every time I felt I was making some progress John would start regurgitating all the mistakes I had made yet again and I would feel myself being pulled back down, having to think about problems I wanted to put behind me, having to defend myself over past actions that I could do nothing about. I found myself resenting him in a way I would never have dreamed possible back on the day we got married. It was as if he had become a different person and I suppose, in many ways, so had I.

Although I liked to think I sheltered them from the worst of the fights, it can't have been any fun for the boys, who were now aged about eleven and seven. The house was too small for any of us to be able to escape the others for long and the bad feelings and raised voices permeated every room. It was exactly the sort of thing I hadn't wanted them to have to put up with in their childhood, as I had had to in mine. But the difference for them was that they did have a choice, an escape route that had never been open to me. In the end Brendan decided he'd had enough of the pair of us and announced, with an incredible display of strength and maturity, that he wanted to go and live with his dad. It wasn't the first time he had threatened me with that one after he'd over-heard a nasty argument, but this time I realised he meant it and that it would be pointless to try to talk him round with promises that John and I would try harder to get on. We had promised before and failed.

I felt very hurt and rejected but I realised with a jolt that he was now old enough to make these sorts of deci-sions for himself and that I should think myself lucky he had such a good dad to go to. I tried to console myself that he would soon see sense, realise the grass isn't always greener and would come back home the first time Rodney laid down the law about something or other. But he didn't. I dare say Rodney, realising he had an advantage and wanting to exploit it to the full as part of his long-term game plan, was making himself as agreeable as possible.

With Brendan at his dad's, enjoying unlimited access to his stepsister and stepbrothers and the rest of Rodney's family, it was now all the harder for Thomas to be stuck at home with us on his own. It wasn't long before he announced that he wanted to go to Rodney too and that was the final straw for me. Despite the effect I knew they were having on the boys, the rows had been getting steadily worse. The police had even been involved on a few occasions and I had taken out injunctions against John. Both the boys made it clear that they no longer wanted to be around John and I realised that I couldn't kid myself things were going to get better on their own. I was going to have to choose between my husband and my sons. When I looked at it in those stark terms there really wasn't any choice – my children were always going to come first.

It was hard for either John or me to let go, but eventually we had to. After Brendan had been staying with Rodney for around six months, John and I broke up and immediately Brendan came back home again. As painful as it was, I knew I had made the right choice because my boys meant everything to me. Being a good mum was my most important job at the time and it came in front of everything else.

Chapter Fifteen

Terry's Wedding

On the 12th of March 1997, my brother Terry was due to get married to his girlfriend, Sharon, and I knew the wedding was going to be an ordeal because Mum and Dad were both going to be there.

It would be the first time they had seen each other since Mum walked out on him, twenty-five years earlier, apparently breaking his heart and ruining his life forever (at least that was what he always told Terry and me). The thought of seeing them together in the same room filled me with horror, awakening every bad and frightening memory I had managed to box away inside my head over the years, but my brother and I had been through a lot together and Terry had always been there for me as a child, so there was no way I would have missed his wedding. I wouldn't have wanted to, as I was keen to mend as many fences in our family as possible, so long as I didn't have to spend more time with Dad than was absolutely necessary.

Dad had offered to pay for the wedding and Terry had accepted out of necessity, so I knew Dad was going to be strutting around the place like the Godfather, soaking up everyone's adoration and gratitude and being the centre of attention, which was what he always enjoyed the most. I hated the idea that he would be making the whole event his own, gloating over all of us. As the day drew closer there were arrangements to discuss and so I couldn't avoid Dad completely, however much I might want to. In many ways it was just like the old times, after Mum first left him. He kept bursting into tears because 'the love of his life' was going to be at the wedding and he 'didn't know how he would handle it'. Seeing this great lump of a man quivering with self-pity like a lovesick teenager brought back memories of all the nights Terry and I had had to listen to his drunken wailings and his frightening promises that he would kill himself if he couldn't get her back, but I bit my tongue and said nothing, determined not to cast any unnecessary shadows over Terry and Sharon's big day.

Despite the fact that Dad had offered to pay for the day, Terry's relationship with him had not been very good recently. I'm not sure exactly what went wrong between them, although I am confident that it was Dad and not Terry who had messed things up. It was a measure of Terry's good nature that he was willing to invite Dad to the wedding despite the bad blood between them, and perhaps a measure of Dad's need to get back into a position of control that he had offered to pay for everything. Money didn't seem to be a problem for Dad as he got older. To start with he was on permanent disability benefits because of his alcoholism, but he had also inherited a bit when his Mum died. She had always adored him and I suspect he got most of the money when they sold her bungalow. On top of that he had whatever extra he could earn with his various activities on the street, living off the immoral earnings of his various girlfriends, just as he always had done.

Still near the edge because of breaking up with John and the aftermath of my suicide attempt, I was becoming more and more nervous about how things would go on the day and I went back on the Prozac tablets, thinking it might help me get through everything. Brendan said he would come along, but Thomas didn't want to. John was invited and said he would like to come, so at least I had two people who should be on my side on the day.

On the morning of the wedding Mum was in just as much of a dither as Dad as she got ready and my brothers and I were running back and forth between the two of them like idiots, checking they were okay, as if we were the parents and it was their big day instead of Terry and Sharon's. With all the fuss you would have thought they were both dressing for a first date. I have to admit, by the time she'd finished Mum did look beautiful. She's still a very good-looking woman and it's not hard to see how she managed to enslave Dad with her looks back when they were teenagers.

The actual ceremony went well, although it felt very odd to see them both in the same place for the first time any of us could remember. Even when we got to the reception at a hotel out in the country it still seemed as if we were going to be able to get through the day almost like a normal happy family. Dad was playing the part of the hero, just as I had known he would, tall and handsome in his suit and tie, filling the room with his presence, shaking hands and hugging everyone, beaming all over his face as if proud of the job he had done as patriarch of this fine family. No one watching from the outside would have suspected just how badly dysfunctional our childhoods with him had been. I dare say anyone who had known, however, would have been able to detect the growing tensions that invaded the room as everyone filled their glasses and started to let their hair down. Dad had brought his current girlfriend with him, which added considerably to the awkwardness. Mum was drinking heavily from the moment we got to the hotel, maybe to calm her nerves like the rest of us. I had also had a few glasses, swallowing them down quickly, unaware that you are not supposed to mix alcohol with Prozac.

The party got under way, everyone started to relax and I actually thought that maybe we were going to get through the whole event without any incidents. Then I saw a sight that made me feel sick, furious and hysterical in the same moment. In full view of everyone, Mum and Dad were locked in a passionate embrace, snogging each other's faces off, apparently unable to resist the magnetic forces that had joined them and then forced them apart so violently over the years. They were sitting together at a table right in the middle of the room, not caring who saw them. His girlfriend watched with dead eyes and didn't look the least bit perturbed. Apparently once put in the same room together Mum and Dad were unable to stay out of one another's arms. I don't think anyone likes to see their parents behaving like that, even if they don't have a family history like ours.

In that split second everything inside my head seemed to explode free of the self-control I had been exercising and I hated my mother more than ever before. I felt a rage growing inside me. How could she bear to touch a man who had repeatedly raped and sold her daughter, let alone kiss him? It was like a thunderstorm erupting in my brain, probably fuelled by the mixture of pills and wine swilling around inside me.

Other family tensions must have been building up in other parts of the room because just as my anger came roaring to the surface I heard raised voices outside the venue. I stormed out, partly to stop myself attacking Mum, and found my youngest half-brother, Adam, fighting with another lad. I didn't bother to find out what it was about, but just piled in as I used to do when I was married to Rodney, letting out all my own aggression and escalating the whole incident horribly. I wasn't really taking in anything that was going on by that stage, overwhelmed by the many different emotions that swirled around in my head on a sea of pills and wine, but I saw John coming striding out of the party and the next thing I knew he had hoisted me over his shoulder and was carrying me back inside like a thrashing sack of potatoes.

My brother Terry, as shocked and confused and over-emotional as me, turned on John for man-handling me and John dropped me so that he could defend himself. Everything had degenerated into chaos and I was as disgusted with myself as I was with the rest of my family but unable to stop the events which were now galloping out of control.

I then fell out with Terry, which still breaks my heart when I think about it. It was his wedding day and I was partly responsible for turning it into a farce. I had provided the wedding cake and I think in my rage and confusion I must have reminded him of that, as if it somehow put him in my debt.

'Take the fucking cake, then,' he shouted back, 'and just go.'

At which point I marched over to the cake, picked it up and hurled it onto the dance floor. I regretted it the moment I had done it and watched in horror as it bounced along amongst the feet of the guests. Turning on my heel I stormed out with absolutely no dignity left at all, hauling a mortified and confused Brendan behind me.

The next problem, which didn't hit me till I emerged into the fresh cool air, was that I couldn't escape under my own steam because we were outside the city, so I then had to phone Rodney and ask him to come and pick Brendan and me up. Why did I always end up having to go back to Dad and Rodney when I messed up my life? Why could I never escape from them completely? Why was I such a complete failure? Of course Rodney loved being the white knight coming to my rescue and he came roaring up in his car within a few minutes.

'What have I told you about that family of yours?' were his first words as Brendan and I bundled into the car, wanting to make our escape as quickly as possible. I hated the fact that Brendan had seen his mother make such an exhibition of herself, but the anger at the sight I had been forced to witness was still boiling inside me, blocking out almost everything else. However hard I tried, I couldn't get the picture of Mum and Dad in that clinch out of my head.

I don't remember where Rodney took us initially, but when we eventually got back to my house, Mum was already there. She was sitting slumped at the table, whimpering on about how Dad was the love of her life, blaming him for ruining everything, soaking in self-pity and completely ignoring everything the two of them had done to their four children, as always. Whatever self-control I had managed to regain with Rodney and Brendan vanished again and I went ballistic, hysterically screaming and shouting exactly what I thought of her, calling her a filthy whore and every name under the sun.

'How could you do it?' I screamed over and over again. 'After everything he did to me? What kind of mother are you?' I think I would have attacked her physically if Rodney hadn't stepped in and restrained me. Rodney the peacemaker once again, the one striving gallantly to unite my warring family.

Afterwards, when I had finally calmed down and slept off the effects of the drink and pills, I felt terrible. Straight away I phoned Terry to apologise for ruining his big day. There were a lot of awful things done that afternoon, but the symbolism of the wedding cake bouncing across the dance floor made my contribution stick out in everyone's memories, particularly mine. John had jumped on the whole incident as fresh evidence that I had screwed up again, that I would never change, but Terry amazed me by being very sweet about it.

'Don't worry about it, Ria,' he said and told me that after I had stormed out of the reception someone had picked up the cake and put it all back together again on its stand.

'If ever you were going to be tested,' Terry said, 'that was going to be it – to see those two together like that.'

I suppose I could put the whole cake-throwing incident down to my inner child having a temper tantrum. I dare say it was a healthy reaction in the circumstances after seeing my parents behaving like that, but apart from having made a scene at my brother's wedding, the worst thing for me was that Brendan was there and had seen me behaving just as badly as the rest of them. I had hoped that observing the whole family together for a normal family celebration would make him feel comfortable and secure, but it hadn't worked out quite how I'd hoped.

Terry and Sharon lived with Dad for a while after they got married, even after they had their little baby girl. Then they had a row about something and Dad rang Terry after a few drinks and threatened to throw their baby out the window of the flat. It was just the sort of stupid thing he would say when he'd had a few, but it was definitely the wrong thing to say to a man who had just had his first baby and adored her beyond anything in the world. Dad and Terry were never reconciled after that.

No matter how much I might try to bring my family together and pretend they were 'normal', Dad would always be able to throw a spoke in the wheel. He was such a huge character that he continued to cast a shadow over all of us long after we had stopped having anything more to do with him.

Chapter Sixteen

A Time to Die

Knowing I had made the right decision about breaking up with John did not help the feeling of failure that enveloped me as my second marriage, which had seemed so perfect at the beginning, collapsed in front of my eyes. I felt completely helpless, and all the sense of empowerment that I had been experiencing suddenly seemed like a complete delusion. As had happened before, my throat started to close up so it was hard for me to speak. Yet again happiness was spinning away out of my reach. Waves of misery overwhelmed me and I found myself slipping back to thinking about suicide as my trump card, the one I could always play when everything else had failed.

The fiasco at Terry's wedding increased my feelings of self-loathing. I heard my father saying 'You're fat and ugly and useless, Ria. No one will ever truly love you but me.' I heard Rodney gloating that no one else would ever want me and that I'd be lost without him and needed him to take care of me. I thought I had been managing to break away from the emotional influence they had over me but now I had failed to hold together yet another relationship. As my depression took hold I began to wonder if Dad had been right all along. Maybe I was the most useless failure in the world and I had been fooling myself to think that I was actually amounting to anything with my attempts at getting an education and my delusions that I was a good mother to the boys.

I had to face the facts; I was thirty years old and I already had two failed marriages under my belt. There seemed no point going back to talk to Marion again because she had done all she could and I was still a useless failure. I was sucked back into a downward spiral that lasted for days. I didn't take any anti-depressants because I was convinced that they didn't work for me and that I was going to have to face up to these demons and fight them on my own, almost as if it was some sort of a test of character. I actually believed I knew better than a qualified doctor; that was how ignorant and stubborn I still was despite all the lessons I had learned in the past.

Gradually I came back to the same conclusion I had reached so many times before: that Brendan and Thomas, and everyone else for that matter, would be better off without me. I decided that it was finally time to admit defeat, to accept that I was always going to be a pathetic, miserable failure and end the struggle, end the pain for myself and for all those around me. The fact that all my previous attempts at suicide had merely resulted in embarrassing failure and guilt-ridden returns to life reinforced my conviction that I was worthless, and also made me all the more determined to get it right this time. I guess many of the previous attempts had been 'cries for help' because once I had taken the tablets I would usually tell someone what I had done. This time I seriously wanted to succeed.

The self-harming incidents had been more about releasing emotions than realistically hoping to bleed to death. On the occasions when I had swallowed sleeping pills, my intentions had always been serious at the moments of swallowing, but had been undermined afterwards by me making a call to someone who could raise the alarm or come to the rescue. The only other time I had been really serious was when I tried to hang myself at the height of my nervous breakdown, but I had still tipped John off about what I was planning to do and had then delayed the act and drunk enough to make myself inefficient, creating a strong chance that I would be saved, even if I didn't realise that was what I was doing at the time. This time I was going to have to be even more careful how I planned it if I wanted to succeed.

There is a beauty spot just a few miles from Norwich called Ringland Hills, which has a reputation for attracting people who want to end their lives. It was also notorious for being the spot where the body of a sixteen-year-old called Natalie Pearman was found after she went missing from the red light district in Norwich in 1992. I thought to myself that maybe she would have understood the desperation I was feeling as I plotted to end my own life. I decided that this would be a place where I could end it all without worrying about being interrupted before I had succeeded.

I waited till the boys were at school and then loaded the car up with everything I would need: my sleeping pills, a litre of wine, a bowl in case I vomited, my bible, pictures of the boys, a duvet and a pen and paper so I could write my farewell letters as I slowly drifted up to heaven, which was how I imagined my exit was going to be.

I drove around the hills for a while until I found what I thought would be the perfect spot to die, parked the car and climbed into the back seat. I felt very peaceful and relaxed now that I had finally made the decision. There was nothing else for me to worry about, no more pain to brace myself for. The story was over. I swallowed the pills, washing them down with the wine, and managed not to be sick. I got out the paper and pen, pulled the duvet over me so I was cosy and comfortable and started writing the letters while I waited for the pills to work, glancing up every now and then at the view, contented and ready to go.

The drowsiness started to come over me and I drifted in and out of consciousness. The letters were written so there was nothing more for me to do. I was in a half-waking, half-dreaming state when I heard a banging noise and a raised voice shouting at me, making my heart thump with shock and my eyes spring open in a sort of mad, unseeing stare. I couldn't work out if the disruption was part of the real world or one last nightmare coming to the surface as I passed through sleep to the next stage. I don't know how long it took to drag myself back to consciousness, but when I got there I was confronted by the angry face of a farmer just a few inches from mine, banging on the car window with his fist and telling me to get off his land.

'This is private,' he shouted. 'You can't park here. Move on!'

Despite the fact that I was trying to end my life, I was still mortified at the thought of upsetting someone and being caught somewhere I shouldn't be, like a naughty schoolgirl reprimanded for having a fag behind the church. Trying to gather my thoughts as best I could from the blur that was filling my head, I clambered and stumbled into the front seat and started the engine. I drove off, blinking hard, opening the window for cold air, trying to stay awake and concentrate on where I was going. I swerved around the countryside for a while trying to find a good place to settle down again and die, but the farmer's angry voice had frightened me and I didn't want to be found and told off by anyone else. In a panic I drove back home, unable to think of anywhere else to go, fighting to stay awake and not have a car accident. The worst thing would have been to have hurt some other innocent person while trying to kill myself; that would have been the ultimate failure. Somehow I made it home without giving in to the urge to sleep, got out of the car and staggered into the house and up to the bedroom with every limb feeling as if it weighed a ton.

I collapsed on the bed and lay there, pleased to be safely home, surrendering to the overwhelming sense of exhaustion and preparing once more to be taken up to heaven and to be relieved of the burdens that still seemed to be weighing my mind down even as I died. The reality of the room around me was slipping away but I didn't seem to be going to heaven as I had hoped. Instead I seemed to be stuck in some ghastly no-man's land, like some sort of other-worldly waiting room. In my semi-conscious dream state, God appeared in front of me.

'Am I dead?' I asked Him.

'You are,' he replied. 'But you can't come into Heaven.'

'Why not?'

'Because you've committed the sin of suicide.' He shrugged as if it was obvious. 'I can forgive you all your other sins, but not this one.'

I must have known that was the case for the vision to come to me, so why hadn't I thought about it until this late stage? Even in my half-dead condition I was horrified. Was I going to be stuck in this no-man's land for all eternity? Maybe I deserved it because of all the bad things I had done in my life. I could feel a pulse throbbing in my leg and was pretty sure that was happening back in the real world of my bedroom. Maybe God was wrong; maybe I wasn't quite dead yet. Maybe he was giving me one last chance to do the right thing. But if so, what was happening to my leg?

Unable to summon enough functioning brain cells to work anything out sensibly, I became convinced that a vein in my leg was on the verge of exploding. I was trapped on this plateau and I was terrified. It was illogical; if I wanted to die anyway, why did I care what happened to my body back on earth? But did I want to die if God wasn't going to let me into Heaven? I needed to pull back and try to work out what I should do, but my brain wouldn't wake up and I couldn't make any of my limbs do as I told them any more. With one enormous effort I managed to pull myself close enough to reality to pick up the phone and call my friend Mel. Although my mouth wouldn't say the words I wanted it to, somehow I managed to communicate to her what had happened and before long the sound of an ambulance siren became part of my hallucinations. I could hear voices approaching through the house and feel hands moving me onto a stretcher. Then I slid away into blackness.

When I woke up and found myself in hospital I was totally despairing. Not only had I failed to end my troubles yet again, but now I was going to have to listen to impatient doctors and nurses telling me that I was taking up time and space which should have gone to genuinely ill people. They had always told me that in the past and I knew they were right. I agreed with them. I had inflicted this on myself and I didn't deserve their kindness or their attention; yet another guilt to carry.

But this time their attitude seemed to be different. After they'd given me charcoal to make me sick and done lots of tests to make sure my condition was stable, a doctor decided I should stay in overnight rather than being sent straight back home as usually happened. I was grateful to him. As long as I could lie in that clean, clinical bed with other people taking responsibility for me, I didn't have to face all the problems and people in the outside world. It was a temporary escape from reality. Although I didn't want to be alive any more, staying in the safety of the hospital was better than going back home on my own to all the chaos and despair, and it was also better than being trapped in limbo, unable to get in through the gates of Heaven.

I knew that if they had let me go home I would only have headed off down the pub and got drunk to try to dull the pain and self-disgust I felt as quickly as possible, which would have made me all the more disgusted with myself when I surfaced once more the following morning, another notch further down the spiral of despair. As long as I was in hospital other people were taking care of me, as if I was still a child, taking care of my physical needs and telling me what to do and what not to do for my own wellbeing. It was a nice feeling and not one I had ever experienced during my actual childhood. I knew Rodney would look after the boys perfectly well while I was gone so that was one less thing to worry about.

I couldn't stop crying as I lay in that bed. I didn't want to speak to or see anyone I knew; I just wanted to lie there amongst kind strangers and weep. There was one particularly wonderful nurse who hardly left my side all through that first night, sitting down beside the bed, talking to me softly and just looking as though she actually cared whenever I opened my eyes.

I wasn't able to keep everyone away. John and my mum turned up the next day, as well as my two best friends – Mel, and a girl called Julie who lived two doors away. They all did their best to say and do the right things, but they only made me feel more guilty and humiliated and more of a failure. Mum and my friends ejected John pretty quickly because I suppose they thought it was all his fault, which of course it wasn't because I was a grown woman now and had to take responsibility for my own actions. It was kind of them to come but I still didn't want to see any of them, I just wanted to die a natural, guilt-free death.

Although I'd been doing so well before, I now sank back down to my lowest ebb ever and to be honest there was a sort of peace to be found in having reached rock bottom, in having finally made up my mind that there was no point in struggling any more. I could understand the feelings of hopelessness that overcame people like John when they could no longer be bothered to even go out of the house, sometimes not even to get dressed. I might not be able to kill myself, but I had still given up on life.

Doctors and psychiatrists came to see me the next day and immediately decided that it wasn't safe for me to go home yet, that I was a danger to myself. I had always tried to avoid being sucked into the mental health system of drugs and psychiatric wards, but it seemed I had no choice now and I was too exhausted to put up any sort of struggle. Everyone else was discussing what would be the best thing to do without consulting me, taking all the decisions out of my hands. In some ways that felt good, allowing me to be a child again, but in others it reinforced my long-held certainty that I was pathetic and useless, that I couldn't even be trusted to take charge of my own life, that I was a burden on everyone. I went from hour to hour like a sleepwalker. I found myself sitting in the psychiatrist's office with my mum and friends and doctors, with everyone talking about me and debating whether I should be sectioned under the mental health act, and I just sat there listening, saying nothing.

The doctors still refused to let me go home unsupervised, but did agree that sectioning me could have detrimental long-term effects on my fragile mental and emotional state. It seemed that many people who are sectioned continue in the cycle of the mental health system with on-going stays in hospital and increasing dependency on prescription drugs. It was agreed that I had done well to avoid all that so far and that it would be a shame to give in now. They all seemed to agree that I had come a long way in the past with Marion's help and that it was only my marriage breakdown that had caused this latest dramatic setback.

To my surprise Mum came to my rescue with an offer to let me stay at her place for a few weeks. Remembering my previous stay there, it didn't seem such a terrible idea. I was touched that she had offered after all that had happened between us and all the things I had said to her on Terry's wedding day. The doctors made her promise that I would be supervised at all times, and they prescribed anti-depressants, which they insisted I took. Despite all the years of anger and resentment that I had built up against Mum for walking out on us as children and never making any effort to improve the family situation, I will always be grateful to her for standing up for me that day.

The boys were staying on with Rodney, so he had to be told what was happening and why I was going to be staying at Mum's. Never one to miss an opportunity, he turned up on the doorstep almost immediately with flowers, chocolates, strawberries and offers of money to Mum for letting me stay there, as if he was still the one responsible for supporting me. Despite the fact that it had been almost five years since I left him, he played the part of the concerned friend to perfection. Mum and I both said how lovely he was to be such a good friend, completely forgetting that he had always said that it didn't matter who I married because I would always end up going back to him, that he would be willing to wait ten years if necessary. He must have thought that with my marriage to John now officially over, his master plan was back on the rails.

I'd feared that Marion might be angry with me when she heard what had happened, but instead she was incredibly supportive, sending me a beautiful bouquet of flowers and a card in which she called me 'God's little princess'.

Chapter Seventeen

self Help

I had only been at Mum's house for a few days before I wanted to go back home and be with the boys. I missed them so much and as my brain returned to the real world I was feeling increasingly disappointed with myself for what I had done. I wanted to be reunited with them as quickly as possible, to try to make up for the sin I had tried to commit, which I could now see clearly would have hurt them more than anyone else. If I had succeeded in killing myself I would have deserted them just as surely as Mum had deserted my brothers and me; there was no excuse for it. Neither of them knew anything about what I had tried to do, or how close I had come to letting them down. Mum and my friends all tried to stop me from going back home too soon, but I knew I was past being a danger to myself, at least for the time being and, I hoped, perhaps forever.

The thing that puzzled me was that with every step forward I believed I had found the answer that would instantly save me from my past. First there had been the birth of Brendan, when a baby of my own was the one thing I had always wanted. Then there was Rodney and the extended family that he brought with him, then Thomas, and Marion and John, and even God Himself. Each one of them had seemed like the answer to all my problems, but none of them had been able to stop me from slipping back into the clutches of a depression that I knew stemmed from the childhood years I had spent with Dad and from my time working on the streets. I still hadn't escaped from Dad.

Eventually the penny dropped that no one thing or one person was ever going to save me.

I was going to have to do it myself.

This revelation hit me like a bolt of lightning during an Easter celebration at Thomas's primary school. I always loved events like that, watching one or other of my boys doing something in front of an audience, glowing with pride and amazement at how I had managed to produce two such perfect little creatures. As I took my seat amongst the other parents in the school hall that day I thanked God that I wasn't sitting in the hospital under section, that I was back out in the world and fighting to survive again.

Thomas came out on stage and read a poem to the hushed audience, tightly clutching a cherished little masterpiece of daffodils, greenery and tin foil in his fist. He looked tall and beautiful, and spoke clearly and confidently. The poem was all about how wonderful his mum was and I felt overwhelmed with a mixture of pride, gratitude and remorse as I listened, unable to stop the tears from welling up. It struck me how different that day would have been for him and for his brother if I had succeeded in taking my life in the car. Instead of proudly reading a poem to his mummy he would have been listening to other children on the stage, knowing that he no longer had a mummy, that she hadn't loved him enough to fight to stay with him. As it was, he knew nothing about all the turmoil in my head and my heart. He just knew that I was his mum and that he loved me – but I was aware that I had very nearly taken his mum away from him. What right did I have to murder this little boy's mummy? It was only thanks to the work of everyone at the hospital that I hadn't broken his heart.

For a moment I was so overcome with revulsion for myself that I felt even worse. Yet again, I thought they both deserved a better deal in life than having me for a mother and that it would have been preferable for them if I had succeeded in killing myself. But even as I was thinking these thoughts I knew I had to stop behaving like this; that I had to break the cycle once and for all. There was nothing I or anyone could ever say that would justify me abandoning these two boys. In a blinding flash of self-revelation I realised that it was only my feelings of negativity and guilt that were destroying me, and that there was no one else to blame any more. As I proudly joined in the enthusiastic applause for Thomas's performance I vowed that I would do whatever I had to in order to make the situation better.

My first step back up the ladder was to re-read the self-help books that Marion had guided me towards, and to do the exercises they contained. I felt I had to find a way of incorporating the concepts of these authors into my everyday way of feeling and thinking about myself and about the things that happened to me. I knew from everything I had read so far that it was my responsibility to save myself, but that to do so I had to learn to love myself and to truly believe that I deserved to be happy.

The things I read opened my eyes to so much of what had been going on all my life without me realising. All day long, for instance, I would be making cups of tea and meals for other people, whether it was husbands or children or just friends dropping in, but I would often reach the end of the day having had virtually nothing to eat or drink myself. I now asked myself why I thought so little of myself that I didn't believe I was worth looking after? I didn't even know what foods I liked, although I could have told you every food that everyone else in the house would or wouldn't ask for. If I didn't value myself more than that, what were the chances of anyone else doing so? If I didn't care enough to look after my own body then I wasn't likely to care about my own happiness either.

Instead of waiting for other people to buy me birthday presents or Valentine presents and then feeling disappointed and rejected when they didn't; why not go out and buy myself a nice bunch of flowers or some perfume that made me feel good? It was a complete revelation to me, taking me all the way back to a Christmas Day when I was a child. Dad was out of prison and Terry and I were out of care, and we were able to spend the holiday like virtually every other family in the country. His girlfriend of the time, Kathy, had made the house look really festive and we were all in the front room on the day handing round presents from under the tree.

I watched as Kathy and Dad gave Kathy's daughter a box, which turned out to be filled with loads of little perfumes, all beautifully packaged. Then they gave each other gifts and as it gradually dawned on me that everyone else had something except me a pain began to grow inside my chest. I forced myself to smile and hold in the tears as I watched all the parcels being handed round and prayed I was mistaken, but still nothing came to me. Dad must have noticed my fixed expression because he laughed and chucked a packet of Maltesers into my lap.

'There you are,' he joked, 'that'll do for you.'

The most hurtful thing was that he thought it was funny to humiliate me in front of the others. He actually enjoyed reinforcing the idea that I was just a piece of shit, not worth any kindness or consideration, not deserving of anything nice, even on Christmas Day. Now, as an adult, I knew I deserved better and I was determined to provide it for myself.

At the same time, it occurred to me that instead of spending so much time hating myself and worrying about how I was going to make myself feel better and happier, I should be thinking of ways in which I could help other people who had suffered from the same sort of problems as I had.

A few weeks after coming out of hospital I went with my friend Mel for a follow-up appointment with the psychiatrist I had seen before. I had gone to a lot of trouble to clean myself up and must have looked very different to the bedraggled, greasy-haired, depressed wreck he had met previously. I explained to him that I knew why I had fallen so low and what I was doing to make myself better, and all the support I had lined up if I got stuck again. As I talked I noticed a smile creeping into the corners of his mouth. For a second I thought he was mocking me, then I got a grip and pushed the negative thought aside, asking him what was so funny.

'I have never seen such an amazing change in a patient,' he said. 'It is so refreshing to hear someone who knows what is wrong with them and what they are going to do about it without having to be led every step of the way.'

'I want to get better,' I enthused, 'and I want to do something worthwhile with my life. I want to find a way to help people with self-esteem and confidence problems, people who find themselves in the same position I was in.'

'That would be a great thing to do,' he agreed. 'You don't need me any more. Go home and get on with your life. Finding a way to help others is a brilliant idea. The system needs people like you, people who understand what it feels like to lose hope but who still manage to find their way back. Do it.'

With that he wished me luck and told me I didn't need to make any more appointments.

Chapter Eighteen

A Promise to Glen

In April 1997, while I was still recovering from the overdose, Mum had her 50th birthday. I was friendly with one of her best friends at the time and we decided to organise a surprise birthday party for her in a local pub. It turned out to be a great evening as I once again attempted to reunite everyone and pretend we were a normal family – Terry, Glen, Chris, me, Brendan and Thomas. It was the first time we had ever all been together for a party and resulted in the one and only sacred photo I have of me and all my brothers together. Although John and I had separated by this time we all made the effort to make it an enjoyable and happy occasion. It wasn't until years later I realised that nobody else in the family ever attempted to organise anything like that. It was always me trying to salvage what I could from our dysfunctional wreck of a family. No one else seemed particularly bothered.

A few weeks after my overdose, Rodney refused to return Thomas to me after a weekend visit. This time it took me almost three weeks to get him back through the courts. Three weeks can seem a very long time when you aren't even sure what the outcome of a situation will be. At that age children are developing so fast that even a few weeks can mean you miss all sorts of changes. I had to hang on very tight to the new philosophies I was trying to live by to prevent myself from giving in to despair or depression.

It was only when I stood back and thought calmly about what was going on that I realised everything Rodney did was a ploy to persuade me to go back to him, to fulfil his long-term plan. He had been certain that I would go back after the suicide attempt in the car, since I wasn't with John any more. He must have been convinced that this time I would see the light and realise how much I needed him. I'm sure he believed that I couldn't manage without having a man around to 'look after' me. When the weeks passed and I grew stronger, he must have realised that it wasn't going to happen, so he went back to using the boys as his weapons against me.

In court he became more proactive in his campaign, declaring that I was an unfit mother because I had tried to kill myself. I think he believed that if he could get permanent custody of the boys I would be forced to go back to him for their sake. He knew I would never want to be parted from them permanently. My solicitor was as shocked as I was when Rodney made the claim out of the blue, and asked the judge for an adjournment while we worked out what to say in response. A quick call was made to the hospital psychiatrist, who instantly agreed to send a fax to the court stating that my suicide attempt had no bearing whatsoever on my ability to care for my sons. I had never abused, neglected or hurt the boys in any way, so there was no reason for the courts to take either of them away from me and give Rodney custody. When the judge read the fax he ordered Rodney to hand Thomas back to me immediately.

That day Thomas had been waiting outside the courtroom with relatives, not knowing which of his parents he would be going home with. When he was told he could come home with me he ran at full tilt across the floor and launched himself into my arms as I came out of the courtroom, almost knocking me off my feet in his enthusiasm, hanging onto me as if he never wanted to let go. My solicitor looked almost as pleased by this evidence that we had reached the right result as I was.

'I don't think I have ever seen such a happy reunion,' she said.

The books I was reading were helping me a great deal to understand the effects of negative thinking and how such habits can be born of negative past experiences. The main focus of the exercises was to help the reader to change self-destructive patterns of thinking and feeling.

It wasn't long before I was hooked on the whole concept. It was such a relief to discover that I could focus on the future instead of always dwelling in the past or struggling with the problems of the present. I was coming to realise that there was absolutely nothing I could do about my past or about the things that Dad and Mum and other people had done or not done to me. What I could do, however, was make the most of the life I had now, and I promised myself that I would do whatever I could to make myself better, both for my own sake and for the boys'.

I continued to see John on and off for about another year after the break-up, and we kept on going to marriage guidance sessions together to see if there was any chance we could salvage the relationship, but my heart was no longer in it. I wanted to move forward, not keep going over and over old stuff, trying to work out why we had made the mistakes we had.

I didn't blame John for pushing me into taking the overdose; it had been completely my decision to swallow those pills. I was an adult and capable of making my own decisions. But I did resent him more generally for letting me down, in a way that made it hard for me to believe I could trust him. I didn't want to spend the rest of my life with someone who made me feel like killing myself. I didn't want to put myself in a position that might lead to me feeling that low again, and I didn't want to put the boys through it either.

Now that I had found them again, and didn't have Rodney there to make things awkward, I had been spending a lot more time with my younger brothers, Chris and Glen. Glen had struggled a bit over the years since I'd been reunited with him. He had had some trouble with drink and drugs, but seemed to have succeeded in getting on top of it. I never knew him to be in a relationship with a girl, but nothing seemed to bother him much. He didn't appear to expect much from life, which can be a healthy way to live for some people.

The foster parents who brought up Chris and Glen must have done a good job to make them so philosophical, but whatever way you looked at it Glen still had a lot of problems. His epileptic fits were getting worse as time went by, making it impossible for him to hold down a job or drive a car. One particularly violent fit had left him lying alone in his flat for forty-eight hours before anyone found him, so he now had to live in a supervised halfway house environment to make sure there was help on hand when he needed it. But he still seemed to have come to terms with the way his life was going to be and didn't appear to be unhappy.

In 1996, when I turned thirty, I had received my first ever birthday card from him, which felt like a major step for someone who had gone through their childhood receiving no cards or presents from anyone in the family, either at Christmas or birthdays. I wanted so much for us all to be reconnected as a family that little gestures like that made a big difference, made me feel we were all moving forward at last. Glen also asked if I would agree to be his next of kin on some form he had to fill out, which I thought was very touching considering the relatively short time we had known one another.

On 13 June, 1997, Chris and I had spent most of the day together and when I received a call from him just half an hour after he left my house, I guessed there must be something seriously wrong.

'It's Glen,' he said, and I knew immediately from his distraught tone that he was going to tell me Glen was dead.

As soon as he got home from my place, he'd had a phone call saying that Glen had died of an epileptic seizure in his sleep. I knew his fits had been getting worse and that he had sometimes been losing whole days to them but I never realised they could have the power to actually end his life. He had been found quite quickly because he lived in the supervised environment, but not quickly enough to save him. He was just twenty-six years old.

Glen's death shocked me and reawakened a lot of the old anger that I had been working so hard to quell. It wasn't so much anger at the injustice of a lovely young man's life being cut so short, as anger towards everyone who had let us down over the years. It seemed to me that Glen had never really enjoyed any quality of life as an adult because of his epilepsy, and that he had deserved a break after the terrible start in life that Mum and Dad had given him.

I didn't know anything about his years in foster care, but I knew how miserably his life had started, before Mum disappeared and he was taken into foster care. I also knew about some of the difficult problems he had struggled with in adult life, particularly his trouble with drink and drugs. I felt angry that we had no family home to take his body to. I remembered the huge family ceremonies after Dick Drake, Rodney's father died, and felt sad that we couldn't do the same for Glen because our family was so fractured.

Chris and I arranged for his body to be taken to the chapel of rest at a funeral home, which is where I went to visit him. He looked so handsome lying in his coffin, just as if he was sleeping. I had never seen him look so peaceful in life, which made me feel doubly sad. It was always impossible to feel scared around Glen, even though he was a giant of a man, because he was so kind and gentle. I felt cheated that I had only just begun my relationship with him and now he had been taken away from us. I felt angry at my parents and at the authorities and at life itself.

As I sat beside him for the last time I held his hand and talked to him, promising him that one day I would write our story in a book so that he would never be forgotten. For weeks afterwards I would wear one of his baggy t-shirts when I wanted to feel close to him, lighting a candle and playing 'Champagne Supernova' by Oasis, which was his favourite song. I liked to believe that we would meet again one day somewhere where we could play together like the innocent children we were never allowed to be.

I guess even Mum and Dad must have felt guilty about the way Glen's life had turned out, but both Chris and I decided that we didn't want them to be involved in organising his funeral. Dad was ready to pay for everything, just as he had with Terry's wedding, but we didn't want to give him the satisfaction of behaving like the big generous patriarch, accepting everyone's praise and gratitude and sympathy. He had never done anything for Glen while he was alive, so why should he be allowed to take the credit for doing something now he was dead?

Neither Chris or I were quite sure how we were going to pay for it, but then to our surprise we discovered that Glen had managed to save up a little bit of money, more than enough to afford whatever was needed. It was almost as if he was sticking up two fingers at the parents who had never done anything for him, showing them that he didn't need them, that he had been able to take care of himself even without their help.

At his funeral, the crematorium was packed with people and we played Oasis songs that we knew he would have liked. I was surprised by how many pretty girls there were there who I had never met before. I wondered how much any of us had really known about Glen's private life. He was a very private man in every way. Seeing so many strange faces was a poignant reminder of how much I wished I had known him better and for longer. I met members of Glen's foster family – brothers and sisters he had grown up with, whom I'd never met before – and they all had wonderful things to say about him. It seemed he was loved and respected by everyone who knew him.

Although Mum and I were a lot closer by that time than we had ever been before, I found it hard to support her through the bereavement. I felt my loyalties lay with my dead brother, who she had abandoned as a baby and shown no interest in after that. I found it impossible to feel sorry for her when she appeared to grieve, and hard to even talk to her during the funeral. She might have lost a son but then she had chosen to hardly know him while he was alive.

Chapter Nineteen

Toni

By 1998 John and I had almost ceased to have any contact with one another and I was getting on with working, studying and finally enjoying my life. My self-confidence was growing every day. I had joined a gym and for the first time in my life I had started to respect and take care of my body, a body that had been used and abused by me and by other people for nearly thirty years. I swam regularly and took up yoga. That didn't mean I had completely given up having fun. I still went on wild nights out with my girlfriends whenever I could, but I no longer had to get blind drunk in order to enjoy myself. Instead I was finding enormous satisfaction in exploring new things and finding out who I really was and what I truly wanted from life.

Financially things were still a bit of a struggle but I would work overtime whenever I could and do car boot sales to make a few extra pounds to get whatever treats the boys might need. I couldn't bear the idea of them going without possessions that their friends took for granted just because I couldn't afford them. That didn't mean that I wanted to indulge or spoil them in any way; I just wanted to give them the sort of childhood I would have liked to have had myself. I imagine that is the goal of most normal parents. John had taught me how to erect a tent and build a campfire, so I took them camping one summer, a six-hour drive away to Newquay in Cornwall. I think it was as much of an adventure for me and my inner child as it was for them.

The jobs I had been taking, in catering and in bars and the Sports Village, had helped a lot in convincing me that I was capable of doing most things if I put my mind to it, but none of them had given me much job satisfaction, merely providing the money I needed to live and the experience I needed to go for other, better jobs. When I went to work in an old people's home for three months, I enjoyed the experience much more. At least I enjoyed the work, if not the internal politics.

I was constantly on the look-out for something that I thought would be really rewarding. When I saw a job advertised to look after a young woman who had suffered from a devastating brain-stem stroke at the age of twenty-one, which had left her severely disabled and wheelchair bound, I decided to apply. I was told that the client's name was Toni and that she needed a team of carers to look after her twenty-four hours a day. I was asked to come for an interview and the moment I met Toni I knew I wanted to work with her.

She was only a few months younger than I was and had two young sons, just like me – in fact her first child had been born at the same time as Brendan. Toni was paralysed from the neck down, with a permanent tracheotomy. She wasn't able to dress or feed herself or do anything much. She could barely speak above a whisper so often I had to lip-read in order to understand what she was trying to say. My job would be to toilet her, brush her teeth, feed her, dress her, clean her tracheotomy, change her catheter, and anything else that needed doing. It was agreed that I would mostly work nights and if she was well she might sleep through, but if she had a problem like a cold she could be up all night.

Although she was severely disabled physically Toni still had all her mental faculties and possessed an amazing determination to make the best of the hand she had been dealt by fate. Watching the cheerful, brave way she faced the terrible challenges each day threw at her made me feel deeply inadequate and inspired at the same time. I enjoyed her company so much I wanted to be with her as much as I could. I wanted to help her, but I also wanted to learn from her as well. I was hired and from the first day it felt more like a friendship than a job.

After spending many years in hospital Toni had been able to move into her own bungalow so that she could be reunited with her sons, and that was why she needed so much help. She was an inspiration in every way – beautiful, cheerful, generous and determined – and made me realise how lucky I was and how precious life was. I felt ashamed for all the times I had tried to end my life while Toni was being forced to fight so hard to cling onto hers.

I first started helping her in 1997 while I was at the very tail-end of my relationship with John. That meant I could work nights, attend my GCSE courses during the day and be with the boys when they got home from school and during the holidays, because John would be there to look after them at night. Once we split up, however, babysitting became more of a problem and I wasn't sure how I was going to cope. I was always determined that I wouldn't become a single parent living on benefits because I wanted to show the boys a different way of living, and I also thought that if I was stuck at home all day watching daytime television I would feel like a failure and might well slip back into depression again. More important than that, however, was the fact that I certainly didn't want to leave Toni. Both my marriages had left me in debt and I had come to realise that if I wanted to achieve anything in life I had to go out and earn it for myself, that I could never rely on anyone else to do it for me.

Luckily my sister-in-law, Chris's wife Sam, offered to babysit the boys for me and the ever-ready Rodney also stepped in to help. At one stage I was doing three different jobs at once in order to get myself out of debt and into a strong enough position to be able to buy my house. Both Rodney and John had talked about buying the council houses we lived in when the opportunities arose, but neither of the marriages had ever been stable enough for long enough periods for us to make such a huge commitment. (Rodney didn't really believe in that sort of thing anyway, having such a low opinion of 'Gorjers'.) Now things were different because I didn't have to rely on anyone else to provide the money or make the decisions; I was the head of our little family and I could do whatever I wanted. I went to the bank to ask about getting a mortgage and, despite feeling completely intimidated the moment I walked through the door, I succeeded. It seemed like the most enormous and empowering achievement imaginable. It felt good to have goals and to be busy all the time, although it was hard work as well.

I worked with Toni for five years, from 1997 to 2002, until her body finally gave up the struggle and she died unexpectedly in her sleep. She stayed around long enough for her boys to become teenagers and not to need her so much any more, and then it was as if she decided she had struggled long enough. Being with her had helped me enormously in my own journey towards an understanding of what true happiness was. There is no time to feel sorry for yourself and no excuse for being selfish when you are with someone who has so much more to contend with but never complains about anything and still retains their joy and excitement about life. She had even enrolled on a computing course to learn how to use a keyboard and she was always up for going out shopping, never wanting to lie around in bed feeling sorry for herself. Her courage put everything into perspective and made me realise that even then I was often still allowing myself to get upset over the most stupid little things when I really didn't have anything to complain about.

When she died I was heartbroken. Not only had I lost a good friend, but I had lost part of my own identity as well. Caring for Toni had become who I was and why I existed, and now she didn't need me any more, I didn't know what to do next. Because she had been such a good friend I didn't feel I could do the same job for anyone else. Unable to think of anything better, I took a post at B&Q just to keep the money coming in for the mortgage while I considered my situation.

Although I was feeling much better about myself by then, I would still have periods when I fell back into depression – usually because of some man in my life who was proving to be yet another disappointment. Choosing suitable men has never been my strong point and I regret that my boys have had to witness so many rows over the years, and have seen far too many men coming and going through their home. I wish now I had been strong enough to live on my own more often and not to be constantly searching for some ideal man who didn't exist.

I sometimes wonder if I would have been a better mother to the boys if I'd had them when I was a little older. Maybe if I had been more mature I would have grown out of needing a man in my life the whole time, regardless of whether he was any good for us or not. There were times when I became desperate with the way things were going and would shout at the boys out of frustration, which they seldom deserved and which might not have happened if I had been a bit older and bit wiser. But it's no good dreaming of what might have been. Despite everything, I know I have brought up two really nice young men and that is all that matters. Whoever else came and went in their lives, as far as they were concerned I was always there for them, and so was Rodney. They didn't know about the suicide attempts until they were old enough to cope with the information, and until I had passed safely beyond that stage of my life. I've loved everything about being their mum, and I make sure they know it at every opportunity.

In so many areas of my life during those later years I was able to act intelligently, independently and success-fully, but then I would go and spoil it all by getting involved with an abusive or dependant man who I would allow to turn my life upside down yet again. It seemed as though my subconscious methods of dealing with my relationships had never really changed. I imagine that if you are betrayed as thoroughly and repeatedly by your father as I was, you are never able to completely fill the void that it leaves in your soul. Maybe, I thought, I'll never be able to trust my own judgements on men, or how to behave in relationships, because the role models I had growing up were so horrific, but at least I have learned how to be happy and fulfilled on my own.

Chapter Twenty

Positive Thinking

Despite my disastrous love life, I was beginning to see myself as a worthwhile human being. My confidence was growing and I was feeling great most of the time. I was learning that positive thinking can create positive experiences.

Even though I wasn't seeing Marion on a regular professional basis, I was still in touch with her and used to attend the annual general meetings of her organisation, Adult Survivors of Incest and Sexual Abuse, in order to show my support. Marion used to invite survivors of abuse to talk about their experiences and their recovery, or she'd get professionals who would talk about the support being given to victims. One year the speaker was a police officer called Terry Lowe, who worked in the child protection unit. I went because I wanted to hear what he had to say about the work he and his colleagues did, wondering how much things might

261

have changed since my experiences with the police twenty years before.

As he began to talk I could feel the familiar stirrings of an old anger inside me. Terry had a soft, warm and caring way about him, which was winning over the audience, and a strong, purposeful presence, which made you think he knew what he was talking about. It would have been easy to trust him but for me his words brought the memories flooding back of how let down I had felt as a child. I had trusted them to protect me and all they had done was make me tell them the gory details of how I had been abused and then let my case drop, leaving me feeling that I wasn't important enough for anyone to do anything to help me. To raise someone's hopes and then dash them is often much crueller than not raising them at all, particularly if that person is already vulnerable.

Most of the police I came across as a child seemed more concerned about the worry I was causing my father than about the damage that was happening to me. One time I was picked up by a CID man when I was soliciting on Ber Street at the age of fourteen. He knew my age and that I was a ward of court, but he was a friend of Dad's and that was his main concern.

'You do cause your dad a lot of problems,' the policeman tutted as he drove me back to Dad's flat. He was talking about Dad as if he was a sweet, long-suffering old man who didn't deserve to have a delinquent daughter, rather than my pimp, the man who had instigated and encouraged everything I had ever done wrong in my life. On the way home he stopped off at the fish and chip shop to get something for us to take for Dad's supper; that made it very clear to me where the sympathies of the police lay. It was little wonder it never occurred to me to go to them for help as a teenager, no matter what happened to me.

A solicitor I knew back in 1992 when I was getting divorced from Rodney suggested that I should sue Dad for the things he had done to me, but I was turned down for the legal aid that I needed in order to go ahead with the case; it was another slap in the face. We then went to the Criminal Injuries Compensation Board and that fell through too. Each time I came in contact with the authorities it meant spending whole days making statements, talking through the same painful memories, living them all over again. But each time it led to another rejection, another confirmation that I didn't deserve any better, that I wasn't worth anything.

As Terry Lowe talked about the importance of a bond of trust being established between the victims and the police I had to fight hard to keep my fury in check and not shout out like some mad heckler.

'It is important that victims come forward,' he said. 'It doesn't matter how long ago the abuse was, they can still mount a prosecution.'

Once he had finished speaking he asked if anyone had any questions and I waited until everyone else had asked what they wanted to, feeling tense with a mixture of anger and nerves as I prepared to speak out. By the time everyone else had had their say and I decided it was time for me to speak, my voice was shaking with emotion and from the effort of staying in control.

'Do you know how devastating it is to trust the police?' I asked. 'To put all your hopes into being protected and supported, and then to have those hopes continually dashed? Can you imagine how crushing it feels to know that some people are given protection when you are not? It would be nice if the system did lock away the monster who had hurt you so badly, but can you imagine how hurtful it is to see them carrying on with their happy lives, oblivious to the hurt and damage they have caused?'

The room fell into an uncomfortable silence. Everyone was avoiding looking in my direction for fear of catching my eye. Terry did his best to answer my mainly rhetorical questions but the atmosphere had been made tense by my obvious anger. I must have sounded as though I was on the edge of losing control and I might burst into tears in front of everyone.

'Could I speak to you after the meeting is over?' Terry asked kindly.

There was enough calm reason left in some part of my brain to know that this was a man who was doing his difficult job as well as he could. My words were really aimed more at the establishment that he represented than at him personally. In my mind I was remembering all the officers who had let me down, brought me bad news or delivered me back to Dad's front door during the years when I really needed their help to escape.

By the time the rest of the audience had filtered out and it was just him and me in the room I had managed to get a bit more self-control, although I was still trembling as I went over to where he was packing up his things. He asked me a few questions about my past and listened to me for a while. I told him about how Dad had abused me himself and how no one had been able to stop him. I explained that in the end he had gone to prison for living off my immoral earnings but not for raping me himself, by which time I was old enough to be almost free of him anyway.

'We could open the case again,' he said eventually. 'We could try to prosecute your dad for incest.'

The idea of having anything to do with Dad terrified me. I had worked hard to make a separate life away from him, but at the same time I felt I wanted to do it. Why should he be allowed to get away with it? No one had ever officially admitted that the incest had happened and I wanted it to be acknowledged and put on record. No one could undo the damage that he had done, but at least they could admit that it had happened.

Terry Lowe came to my house a few days later and went through the whole sorry saga of my childhood again. It took an entire day of me talking and him listening and gently prompting me with the occasional question. It had been a long time since I had described my early life experiences to anyone apart from Marion and it was painful to be turning over all the memories that I had carefully reburied back out of sight. As they reared to the surface like zombies in a sort of mental graveyard they brought with them all the anger and sadness again, although because of the work I had done with Marion I was much better at coping with the emotions this time round. It was still like having to live through the whole experience again and I wondered if it was going to be worth it. How many times can you go through something, trying to get some recognition from the world of what you have had to put up with, only to have it thrown back in your face again? I had asked Leigh, a friend I had met on a course a couple of years earlier, to be there too and her presence was an enormous help and support. The more I thought about it, the more I wanted this prosecution to go ahead and to succeed, and for Dad to be made to face up and pay for what he had done to me.

Terry Lowe was brilliant and as optimistic as he could be, but he had to keep warning me that because of the length of time that had elapsed he might not be able to persuade the Crown Prosecution Service to proceed on my behalf. I heard all his warnings, but still my hopes were rising.

At the end of a gruelling day Terry went off saying he would do the best he could and let me know what happened. It was hard to get my mind to settle back down into the routines of normal life after having had the mud all stirred up once more. A few weeks later Terry phoned to say the CPS were not prepared to take the case to court. They said the whole case was too complex because so much had happened in the past, all of which would have to be brought up and gone through again.

It was another rejection, but I must have come on a long way since I was a teenager because I wasn't as disappointed or angry as I had feared I might be. I was just pleased that Terry had thought I was worth taking the time and trouble over. I knew he had done his best on my behalf and he sounded as disappointed by the result as I was.

'We could still apply to the Criminal Injuries Board for compensation,' he suggested. 'I'm sure you have enough evidence to pursue it and you don't need to have a criminal conviction in order to pursue a claim.'

I explained that I had been down that route before, first through suing Dad and then going to the Criminal Injuries Board. Both claims were rejected, adding yet more fuel to my certainty that I was a worthless person and that nobody cared about what had happened to me. Terry's confident tone made me feel much more positive, even though he warned me that it could be up to eighteen months before we got to hear anything. I decided to let him try again. What did I have to lose?

All the reading and the thinking I was doing were genuinely helping me to learn how to love myself and to love life in a way I don't think I would ever have managed under my own steam. One of the exercises I found most useful was to write down positive affirmations and quotes and stick them up around the house in places like the fridge or kitchen cupboard doors – things like 'I am good enough' and 'It's not I can't, it's I won't'. The idea was to give myself constant reminders to keep it up and stay positive. The problem with that was that the notes were on permanent display for anyone who happened to come round to the house. If they saw one of the books, most of my friends didn't take much notice and they certainly wouldn't bother to open it up and study it. But if anyone sees a short note or homily stuck up on a wall or a fridge it is hard to resist reading it and a lot of the people who came to my house weren't able to understand what it was all about. If I tried to explain they would ridicule me for being some sort of new age nutter, which hurt more than I was willing to let on because I wanted so much to believe that there was a better way of living than the one I had been brought up with.

I had to keep reminding myself that it didn't matter what other people thought; positive thinking was working for me and that was all that was important. Because of reading these books I felt better and was enjoying being single for the first time in my life. I didn't need, or even want a man in my life to rescue me or protect me. I was managing just fine on my own. I was disappointed that I couldn't share my discoveries and enthusiasms with my friends, especially as many of them would have benefited from some positive thinking themselves. It would have been nice for us to have been able to talk about things as a group, but I had to accept that they weren't interested or that perhaps they had some deeper personal reasons for not wanting to go there.

There are always people who want to hold you back, and they are often the people you think of as your best friends. If I bought a copy of the *Daily Mail* there were some people who would tell me I was putting on 'airs and graces' because they knew I used to read *The Sun*, just like them. People are scared of change. They want you to stay the way you were when they first got to know you and find it hard to adapt – but the very best friends will always manage to support you whatever you do.

After I got my sociology GCSE, I went on to take a psychology course through the adult education system. To be honest I went a bit 'course mad' for a while, having discovered how much there was out there that I could do, and anxious to prove to the whole world that I was as good as everyone else, that I could do all these things if I wanted to. I even took a counselling course, wondering if that might be something I could pursue as a profession in order to help other people, as Marion had done for me. In the end, although I really enjoyed the course, I decided counselling wasn't for me. I had too many strong opinions and I feared I wouldn't be able to resist voicing them to my patients, which is something a counsellor should never do. You are meant to patiently guide clients until they come to their own conclusions.

The course was interesting, though, and taught me a lot about listening skills, showing me how little I was listening to other people, as well as how little they were listening to me. I realised it was particularly true with the boys. It is easy to get into bad habits with children, sending them messages through our body language and lack of eye contact that tell them we are not interested in what they are saying. I observed a group of mothers gathered outside the school gates at pick-up time. We were all chatting when the kids came rushing out to find us, bubbling with excitement and wanting to tell us all about their days or to show us some work of art they were proud of, and we hushed them up and kept talking to one another. It would have been so easy to spend a minute or two showing an interest in them at that moment, but instead we were teaching them that what they had to say was not of importance. I realised that parents are doing it all the time, even the good ones, and I felt guilty for all the years when I hadn't realised what a poor listener I was.

I got on particularly well with my psychology tutor, Anne, who was also involved with courses that empowered women and was interested in the same self-ethos that was now fascinating me.

'Why aren't they running any self-empowerment courses here?' I asked her at the end of class one day.

'I don't know,' she said. 'They should be.'

I went away and thought about it and decided that rather than complaining no one was running a course for people who were in the same position I had been in just a short time before, I should get on and write one myself, drawing on all the lessons I had learned from the books that Marion had guided me towards. It is an indication of how my confidence must have grown by then that I even thought I could do such a thing, never mind actually sitting down and writing a twelve-week course entitled 'Improve your Self Esteem'. My only qualifications for writing such a course was a hundred per cent belief in my work and an absolute passion for the goals I was hoping to achieve. I wanted to help other people who were trapped in the self-destructive cycle of negative thinking that I had been through, and to share everything I had learned.

I'd had to train myself to think positively and I was sure I could pass the same techniques on to other people. Instead of using phrases such as 'I can't' or 'I should', for instance, I now made myself say 'I won't' and 'I could'. Instead of thinking 'I *should* go and visit my Nan in hospital' and then feeling guilty that I didn't, I would say 'I *could* go and see my Nan in hospital'. That way it became a conscious choice whether to go or not to go and a much stronger statement. I wouldn't feel guilty and I would be more likely to do what I needed to do.

It was all about taking control of my own destiny, deciding what was the best thing to do and then doing it, rather than passively allowing events to happen to me. It was totally changing the way I felt about myself. Instead of always saying 'It's not my fault' I had to start thinking 'I'm totally responsible'. I had needed to learn that life was not so much a struggle, as I had always believed it to be, but was actually a great adventure.

Whereas once I would look in the mirror in the morning and immediately think that I was too fat, or that I had a grey hair or a spot, perpetuating the idea that no one would ever be able to love me, I discovered that if I told myself I was gorgeous that would immediately make me feel better. As a result of feeling better I would become more attractive and interesting to people around me and they would raise my spirits further by the way they reacted towards me. In the past if I knocked over a cup I would automatically tell myself off, calling myself a 'stupid cow', when actually it was just a silly little accident and not even worth bothering about.

I was succeeding in training myself to think the right way, but I longed to be able to share all the ideas that so excited me with other people. These were the sorts of lessons that many of my friends believed were laughably simplistic and naïve, but I had tried them and discovered that they definitely worked. I had found I was capable of doing things that I had never imagined for a moment were within my capabilities. Now I was ready for one more challenge.

Chapter Twenty-one

Becoming a Teacher

Towards the end of 1998 I went to Spain on holiday with a casual boyfriend. It was the first time I had ever been abroad in my life and although I had a great time, I hated being parted from the boys for even a couple of weeks, and kept wishing they were there to share the experience with me. John and I had often talked to them about all of us travelling abroad as a family, even going as far as looking through brochures with them and getting all excited, but we had never actually managed it because of the cost and because of our various ups and downs. However, the moment I got back home from this holiday, bubbling with excitement about the whole experience, I promised Brendan and Thomas I would take them with me next time and I knew that I truly meant it. I regretted the fact that I had left it so long before going anywhere outside England and I wanted the boys to have the experience of seeing something of the world.

Looking back now I don't know how I managed to scrape together the money, but I guess it just goes to show what you can achieve if you set your heart on something. It was at moments like that when I regretted not having the sort of parents who would help out. For instance, it would have been so nice if the boys had a granddad who would slip them a bit of extra holiday spending money or who would offer to run us to the airport to save us the cost of a taxi. But there had never been any chance of me letting Dad near the boys when they were small and I wasn't about to give him the satisfaction now, so that was the price we all had to pay.

Six months later I was back at the airport with Brendan and Thomas, preparing to catch another flight to Spain and feeling so proud of myself. A few years before I would have only seen the difficulties and dangers of going abroad with two young boys without a man to help, but I had learned through Marion and the books I had read and the courses I had been on that you can't live your life like that. If you only see the problems and always think negatively, you never achieve anything. At some stage you have to decide what you want from life and then you have to go for it, ignoring the negative little voices in your head, which will always be trying to persuade you that it is 'too expensive', 'too difficult to organise' or 'too dangerous' to attempt on your own.

As we boarded that plane in the middle of the night on our great adventure together, it seemed to me that I wasn't useless after all. I had actually achieved something better for my boys than the life our parents had given my brothers and me. There were still times when I felt very alone and scared as a single mum (especially in an airport in the middle of the night), but the positives now far outweighed the negatives. Once we reached our destination and I saw how much the boys enjoyed the whole experience, I felt very proud of myself for having done it.

When we returned to England I found a mountain of messages waiting from Terry Lowe, the friendly police officer, asking me to ring him. The neighbours told me that a man had been calling at the house trying to find out where I was but refusing to tell them why. It turned out that the mystery man was Terry and he wanted to inform me that the Criminal Injuries Board had accepted the claim we had put in and they were offering me £15,000 compensation for the damage I had suffered as a child.

I was overjoyed for loads of different reasons. To start with, it was proof that someone in an official capacity was finally believing me and recognising the seriousness of what I had been through. This was concrete proof that Dad had been wrong to do what he did to me and someone actually thought I was worth compensating.

I sometimes wonder if I succeeded this time where I had failed before because I needed to believe that I was worth something myself before I was ever going to be able to convince anyone else. There is a school of thought that says you need to be able to love yourself before you will be able to love anyone else, and I guess that applies to other areas of life too. As long as I accepted my father's opinion that I was useless, I was giving off a vibe that made everyone else think the same about me but by the time I met Terry I had begun to believe that I had some self-worth.

Once the initial euphoria wore off and I thought more deeply, it did seem as though I was being offered blood money. It was a lot of cash – I understood that – but what price could anyone put on a young girl's virginity? In some ways I felt it was a bit of a pay-off and, when you viewed it like that, it wasn't nearly enough. But then no amount of money would ever truly compensate me for what I had been through during those years that I was in Dad's power. At a realistic level, £15,000 was a very useful sum (particularly for someone who had just paid for her first-ever family holiday abroad), and helped us a lot. I felt pleased that I had managed to buy my own house and take the boys on holiday under my own steam before I even knew that the money was coming. They would not have seemed like such great achievements if I'd had to rely on the compensation to fund them. It seemed to support the idea that if you make the effort to help yourself in the first place, other good things will follow.

The compensation money enabled me to make some much-needed improvements to the house and to have laser surgery to remove some of the tattoos I had been so ashamed of for so many years. I had the one saying 'Dad' removed from my left wrist; on the right, 'Property of Brian' was too big to remove completely so I had it turned into a pretty black rose. Then I removed all the awful homemade ones I'd done while in the care home at Bramerton – a heart on my ankle and three or four messy ones on my arms. It was wonderful to see them disappear but I was still left with the embarrassing scars on my arms where I had cut myself so badly in moments of despair.

My divorce from John came through in May 1999 and of course I felt hurt, and embarrassed to think that it was my second failed marriage, but I was determined not to feel like a failure myself, or to get caught up in another spiral of negativity. I kept my eyes firmly on the future and concentrated on setting up my Self-esteem course at the adult education centre.

It was to be a ten-week course of two-hour sessions. First I showed what I had written to Anne, my psychology teacher, who had become a good friend. I felt absolutely passionate about the subject and watched nervously as she scanned through the pages, glancing up to look at me every so often before going back to her reading. Living on council estates all my life I had seen so many young single mothers struggling with life, and I believed they would all benefit from being taught the basics of how to attain some self-respect in order to begin the process of fighting back against the many forces that constantly undermined their confidence, usually starting with their partners but often including the very agencies that were meant to assist them. All the time I was hearing about girls who were suffering from depression or had trouble with drink or drugs or were living in abusive relationships and I wanted to tell them about the ideas and lessons that had helped me to feel better about myself and break the cycles of destructive behaviour.

I could see these girls every time I stepped outside my front door – heads down, their appearances uncared for, their expressions partly reflecting their anger with the world and partly their fear, weighed down by children as they struggled to do the right things and to resign themselves to their fate. They looked so sad, just plodding on in the footsteps of their mothers and grandmothers before them, not having anyone to show them that there was a better way to approach life, to tell them that they deserved more.

'I think it's absolutely brilliant,' Anne said eventually. 'You should send it off to adult education and see if they would be interested in letting you set it up.'

Her praise set my heart racing. I had been worried that perhaps I was deluding myself that I was capable of writing something like this, but if Anne liked it then maybe it was okay. If so, then I was actually creating something; actually achieving something worthwhile. I might even be able to help other people. I was no longer the useless child and woman that I had always been told I was. I sent the proposal document off and the adult education authority accepted it, agreeing to put it on the curriculum. The course was called 'Improve Your Self-esteem'.

The one catch was that a person needs to have some self-esteem already in order to even think of enrolling in such a course. If you are deeply depressed, with no sense of self-worth, you probably won't even walk in through the doors of an adult education centre, let alone put your name down for something that will involve you talking about yourself and your life to complete strangers. So on the first course we only had about six students, but in fact that suited me quite well. It would have been intimidating to have had a big audience the first time I stood up to speak in public. I also thought there was a better chance I could help them when there were so few people to get round. I would have time to get to know them more thoroughly and find out what their individual needs and problems might be, to make the whole experience more personal.

I wanted to avoid hearing too much about the life events that had led to my students feeling they needed to enrol on a course like mine. They had nearly all started out with terrible childhoods and had gone on to be in abusive relationships but I wasn't qualified to counsel anyone. It didn't matter so much why they were the way they were and why they felt as they did. What was important was that they were shown the power positive thinking could have to give them a better and happier future. I didn't want to go in search of their 'inner children', as Marion had with me. I wanted to help them see that by making changes to their ways of thinking they could reap immediate and practical benefits, whatever their past trials and tribulations. Within a group of this sort, if everyone is talking about their pasts it can lead to a dynamic in which they are trying to outdo each other by showing that they had a worse time than everyone else, which can lead to the sort of negative thinking that was the exact opposite of what I was trying to achieve with them.

Most of the people who turned up at the courses were young mums, exactly the sort of people I had been hoping to reach. Many of them had kids who were old enough to be in school, which had given them a bit of time and freedom but had also made them question what they were doing and where they were going as individuals. If a woman has only seen herself as someone else's mother for a number of years it can be a terrible shock when that child no longer needs her and her whole sense of identity can crumble as a result.

The course went so well that I started looking around for other organisations I might be able to work with. There is nothing like a little bit of success to feed your confidence. I got in touch with the Workers' Educational Association, an organisation devoted to adult education, and spent the next five years running the same courses for them. I also started working with people suffering from mental health problems such as depression. These were people from all walks of life who had suffered breakdowns because of divorce or abuse or redundancy or illness or bereavement. A few of them were teachers, cracking beneath the strain of the requirements that the education system put them under.

Even when the courses started to get more popular, I still tried to keep the classes to ten people or fewer. Attendees would generally arrive at the classes with a reasonable knowledge of what self-esteem and confidence are, and they would understand that they were lacking in them, but they tended to believe there was nothing they could do about it, especially if they had mental health problems. They would often feel stuck in their ruts and would find it hard to believe they could move on, however much they might want to. The fact that they were there at all, however, meant they had taken the first step. There were sometimes a few who would argue vehemently that it wasn't going to work, but that could help to stimulate class discussions. I did come across some people who I realised didn't actually want to get better, as they were too comfortable playing the system. There are a surprising number of advantages to being depressed – to start with it can be an excuse to stay 'on the sick' and not do anything with your life – but most people really do want to change. Any initial scepticism amongst the attendees had usually lessened by about halfway through the first session, the final traces evaporating during the coffee break.

One of the first exercises I got my students to do was to write ten things that they believed were good about themselves. It was the same exercise that I had found so difficult when I started my sociology course, when the only thing I could think of was that I was good at frying eggs – so I knew most of them would find it very hard. In the old days, if I had tried to write 'I'm good at being a mother' my head would have filled with all the mistakes I had made over the years, but in the course of building my self-esteem I had come to realise that I really was a good mother. Most people find it difficult to think of ten things but now I can write hundreds: a good mum and worker, trustworthy, patient, a good driver, a good friend, honest, caring, ambitious, good listener, and on and on. For each of those qualities I could also think of examples of things I have done that could prove I wasn't good at them – the negatives instead of the positives. But by training myself to ignore the negatives, I can actually start to love myself and be proud of some of my achievements.

To illustrate how easily self-confidence can be destroyed from an early age I talked about the way we are all treated as children. If a baby is starting to walk and keeps falling over, for instance, the good parent will keep telling her that she is doing well and encouraging her to try again. If the parent screamed at the child, telling her that she was stupid and that she was failing and that she was never going to get it right, the child would pretty soon stop trying at all. Many people suffer that level of abuse all through their lives. It might come from their parents, from bullying by other children, from teachers, partners or employers. I know all too well that if you are told you are useless often enough you will end up believing it is true.

I'll never forget the first time I fell pregnant while I was in care, when I was desperate to have a baby of my own. I was delighted when I found out that for the first time ever I was going to get something that I wanted so badly. It wasn't long, however, before other people started to undermine my joy and make me wonder if I had done the wrong thing.

'The best thing you can do for that child,' one of the less sympathetic staff told me, cruelly puncturing my bubble, 'is have an abortion. You'll always be an unfit mother and that baby's life will be a nightmare.'

I immediately felt sure she must be right, because that was what I had always been told about myself. I didn't go for an abortion but I had a miscarriage not long after which left me feeling devastated.

The triggers for low self-esteem can be varied. Someone who has worked all their lives and suddenly finds themselves out of work and claiming benefits might feel completely humiliated, seeing it as tantamount to begging. But they are focussing on the negatives and forgetting all the years when they did work and support themselves. Another person can find that their self-esteem has been sabotaged by a doctor who obviously believes they are malingering and makes some casual comment like 'Here we go again', when they start to describe their symptoms. Or there could a boss who doesn't believe a sick note is genuine. It might even be your children who keep telling you what a 'crap mum' you are. Kids can be so cruel, especially when they're not getting their own way.

During the session I would have a whiteboard with the word 'me' in the middle and then I would ask class members to come up and write the names of people who have put them down. As the board fills up with words and names it starts to seem unsurprising that the little 'me' in the middle of it has been made to feel bad.

Another of the exercises I would do with them was 'the grid of life', which I learned about in a wonderful book called *Feel the Fear and Do it Anyway* by Susan Jeffers. So many people put all their eggs in one basket. We become completely obsessed with the relationship we are in or the job we are doing, neglecting all the other areas of our lives. What happens then is that when something goes wrong with that relationship or we lose that precious job, our whole lives seem to have come to an end. We no longer know who we are or see why we should continue existing. Someone with a healthy 'grid', however, will have many different boxes. Their relationship will be in one box, their job in another, their family in another, and then all the things they like to do, such as gardening or reading or travelling or being with friends, will be in additional boxes.

The point is to embrace each of the things in the boxes at the time you are doing them. If you are with your family, then totally embrace that experience and don't see it as a chore taking you away from something else you would rather be doing. I had trained myself to think like this while I was working with Toni. When I was with her it was her time and I would concentrate all my attention on her. It wasn't a selfless act because I would end up feeling enormously enriched and satisfied by every encounter with her, when I might have resented the time I was missing with the boys or become frustrated by the many things she was unable to do for herself. By approaching them positively, my times with Toni became among the most rewarding of my life.

If one of those boxes in the grid goes wrong then there are still many others that will keep us going while we try to regain our balance, making us happy at least part of the time, and saving us from falling into any pits of despair. For the grid system to work, however, you have to believe that you matter, that your job and your other interests are all important.

Co-dependency is a big contributor to low self-esteem too. If someone is in an abusive relationship with an alcoholic or with someone on drugs, they need to recognise why they stay there, or why they keep going back. Rather than seeing yourself as a martyr or a victim you have to accept that in a situation like that you are part of the problem. By staying with them or going back to them you are enabling them to remain the way they are. You are as dependent on the relationship as the addict is. You can have a co-dependent relationship with your parents or your children or a boss, just as easily as with a partner.

I would cover listening skills in the sessions as well, and then assertiveness skills. Assertiveness seems to me to be one of the most important life skills anyone can master. All too often in the sort of families that many of my students came from, it would be confused with aggression, which is something entirely different. It had been the same for me when I was in the various care homes I was sent to as a teenager. They were tough places where anyone who wasn't assertive would end up being bullied and victimised. Unable to assert myself at that time because of my lack of self-esteem, I would protect myself with aggression instead. The time when I attacked another girl and cut her hand with a piece of broken glass was triggered by my desperation to stay in control in any way I could. Sometimes assertiveness is just a question of deciding what your position is and then sticking to it, even if it means you end up sounding like a broken record.

There was a woman on one of my courses who was being bullied by her boss, who didn't like the fact that she was taking time off work because of depression. His bullying was making her depression worse, creating a vicious circle and a downward spiral. She needed to decide what it was she wanted to achieve in her dealings with him and then refuse to let him talk her out of it by simply repeating her goals over and over in her head. I think the course helped her to do this. I loved every second of it especially the moments when I could see that I was actually helping my students.

One day as I was driving home from one of my courses, it occurred to me that I was being a little bit of a hypocrite. I'd undergone a number of courses of laser treatment on my tattoos by then and most of them had gone, which I was happy about, but it occurred to me that if I loved myself enough, why would I need to make myself appear perfect to the rest of the world? Where would the vanity stop? By having my tattoos removed was I sending the message to my students that they should have theirs removed too, before they could be accepted by society? Would I have to erase all the physical scars from my past, be a slim size ten, have surgery on the rest of my body before I was ever going to think myself acceptable? It was another break-through revelation for me. Of course with the benefit of hindsight I wish I had made other choices at various times in my past, but those scars are part of who I am and if I love myself I have to love both the good and the bad.

I did some voluntary work as a befriender for a lady with mental health problems who used to self-harm terribly. Her scars were much worse than mine. It would break my heart to see her abuse herself so badly and I wasn't surprised when she confided that she had been sexually abused as a child.

Seeing my students grow through the courses gave me a sense of satisfaction almost as great as the one I got when I looked at Brendan and Thomas and saw how well they behaved towards other people, vindicating many of the decisions I had made during their childhood, particularly the decision to leave Rodney. All in all, when I looked around I felt incredibly proud of what I was achieving.

Chapter Twenty-two

Thoughts on a Spanish Beach

Although I loved teaching the self-esteem courses, they didn't pay enough to support me full-time. I soon found the job I had taken at B&Q after Toni died wasn't enough to satisfy me, and with my newly won self-confidence I moved to a job as a hotel manager. I was actually very good at it but it wasn't long before I was working seventy- or eighty-hour weeks and I could tell I was becoming too stressed because my throat was starting to close up again, just as it had when I'd had my previous nervous breakdowns.

The fact that the job was having that effect on me made me realise I was still not on quite the right path. I remembered how wonderful the few holidays I'd had in Spain had been and began to consider selling up in England and moving down there permanently to start a completely new life in a place where the weather would be warm and the cost of living low. The only problem was Brendan and Thomas, who were now aged nineteen and sixteen; there was no way I would ever have wanted to be that far from them so I decided I would talk them into coming too.

I did everything I could to persuade them both that we should all go together, but they weren't having it. Both of them had discovered the joys of drink and girls by that stage and neither of them wanted to give up their social lives in the city they had lived in all their lives to go on some madcap foreign adventure with their mother. It was beginning to look as though they were the sensible grown-up ones in the family.

I decided to go down to Spain for a while on my own anyway, just to spend some time thinking about what I wanted to do next and as part of the whole healing process. I went out of season, in February, when I knew it would be both quiet and cheap. Although it was what I wanted to do, I felt very guilty about leaving the boys. When I told them I was going they were very encouraging, welcoming the idea of being able to look after themselves for a while and of having the house to themselves. I also knew that Rodney would be around if they encountered any problems, but I still missed them from the moment I boarded the plane and wished they could be there to share the experiences with me.

I spent a month living in Benidorm, a place I already knew and loved, feeling a bit lost and alone as I asked myself questions about where I wanted to go for the next stage of my life. All I could think was that I wanted to write a book about what had happened to me as a child, just as I had promised Glen when we were alone together in the chapel of rest. I had held off doing it for as long as the boys were still at school because they knew nothing about my past with Dad, or about me working on the streets, and I didn't think it would be fair on them to tell the whole world about it until they had left school. Other children can be very cruel and I didn't want them to have to suffer unnecessarily because of what had happened to me. But now they had grown up and I felt I had enough time on my own to have a go.

Once I started thinking about it I couldn't stop and I would find that at night I would lie awake in bed, unable to get to sleep because of all the ideas buzzing around in my head, begging to be committed to paper.

When people hear the name Benidorm they tend to think of nightclubs and cheap package hotels, but there is much more to the town than that. The old part is beautiful and has lots of history. It is fun to see the nightlife, but that isn't really what Benidorm is about. I felt really safe there. During the days I took long walks along the beach, chatting away to God and myself. In the evenings I would go to the bars and restaurants. I made good friends down there and although I was desperate to get back to Brendan and Thomas I was still in tears on the night before I was due to leave, part of me not wanting the experience to end.

I wanted to sell my house in England and come straight back to Spain as soon as I could, if I could just persuade the boys what a fabulous idea it would be to come with me. Once I got home, of course, it wasn't so simple and they still weren't having any of it. Although I think it would have been a great adventure, I suspect they were probably right. Maybe I was just searching for escape from the past yet again, and it's good to live in a place where you have roots, even if those roots come with some bitter memories.

I came back from my month's break with renewed energy and, with several GCSEs already under my belt, I decided to sign up for an A Level in English, which really started to develop my interest in books and poetry. It was amazing to realise that I was good enough to be able to read and understand serious literature, and I looked for ways to take my studies further while at the same time starting work on my own book about my childhood. I would soon find myself becoming obsessed by the memories for several days at a time and the only way to release them was to write them down.

After passing the A Level, I decided that I wanted to take my education to another level. Education, I believed, was the most effective escape route possible, so in 2007 I enrolled for a degree in English Literature and Cultural Studies at Norwich City College. I no longer felt that I had to prove anything to anyone; I actually wanted to do the course for its own sake. I wanted to be a student, and to experience different worlds and cultures: the academic world, the literary world, all these places that I had believed I could never travel to because I was too stupid and worthless.

All the while I continued writing my own memories and thoughts about my childhood, thinking about everything that had happened to me and especially the time when I worked the streets. In the last two months of 2006, I was seriously shaken up when I listened to the unfolding news about five young women who had been murdered in the Ipswich area. All five had been drug users and all five had resorted to selling their bodies in order to earn the money they needed to buy their drugs each day.

Steve Wright, the man who was arrested, tried and found guilty of murdering them, originally came from the neighbouring town of Norwich, my own hometown. His victims also came from a world I know only too well. Girls from Ipswich would often work on the streets of Norwich if the police were clamping down in their own area, and vice versa. I could picture exactly what the lives of these women must have been like for them to be willing to climb alone into the car of a strange man.

Initially the media was full of headlines about 'five prostitutes', building the story up just as they once built up 'the Yorkshire Ripper' and other serial killers who pick on vulnerable women, but then some of the more thoughtful journalists started to question that approach.

Why were these girls all being lumped together like that? Why was it so relevant that they were working as prostitutes at the moment they met their deaths? Was it not more relevant that they were all young, vulnerable women who were already being exploited even before the sinister figure of Steve Wright crossed their paths? Was it not more important to ask what social forces had led five attractive girls to put themselves in such a terrible position? How come they had been so robbed of their self-esteem that they cared so little for their own safety? There were doubtless a variety of reasons and there were probably differences between the girls, but I suspect not many. Most of us follow this path for a mixture of the same reasons. So if, as a society, we know what leads to these disasters happening, why are we not doing more to change things?

I heard on the grapevine that my dad had been interviewed by the police investigating these murders. He is a man who has lived in that world virtually all his adult life, a man who sees nothing wrong with using girls, however young, as sex objects and potential sources of income. He believes that every girl 'is sitting on a goldmine' and that rather than 'giving it away for free' she should be selling it. One of the main reasons that he believes this is because he has always needed a steady stream of easy income to buy alcohol. There is nothing much easier than getting someone else to sell their bodies and then give you the money, which is what he somehow managed to talk virtually all the women in his life into doing. All his friends were from the worlds of prostitution, alcoholism and drug abuse and most of the ones I knew as a child are dead now from a mixture of different causes.

There is still a class of people in Britain who die young because they are never shown how to look after their physical and mental health and safety. They are never taught to respect or love themselves, so they are never given any reason to want to be careful. They believe they don't deserve any better so they try to escape from reality with the help of drink and drugs or gambling, which means they end up needing more money and are forced to turn to crime or selling their bodies in order to feed their habits and addictions. The problems virtually always stem from whatever happened to them when they were children.

I was born into that world and many of the people I have met and travelled with on my journey have had their lives fall to pieces or have ended up dead. Although a lot of them are killed by drugs, drugs aren't the root cause of their downfall any more than the broken razor blade they might use to slash their wrists; they are just another of the symptoms of the problem like drink, violent and abusive relationships, and self-esteem so low they don't feel they will ever be worthy of being employed by anyone or of being loved by anyone.

I could so easily have met the same fate as those five girls in Ipswich, and it shocked and upset me horribly to read their stories in the newspapers. It was just luck that kept me alive through those early years, but I have also been lucky enough to find a path out of the world that I was born into and that I remained trapped in for so many years. I have been able to get away from the unhappiness and the downward spiral that low self-esteem leads you into. It took me a very long time to find the path but it is one that is open to anyone who has the desire to look for it. Following it was the only hope I had of ever escaping my father and his influence on my early life.

In 2006, Brendan and Thomas both met wonderful partners and moved out to set up their own homes. At first I was nervous that they were going into serious relationships so young, but they have made me proud of the considerate ways they treat their partners. It makes me glad that I made the decisions that I did, that I showed them there are better ways for men to behave towards women than the ways in which they saw Rodney and other men of my generation treating me. They are both truly 'gentle' men, and I feel proud that they have escaped from the world inhabited by bullying, controlling, abusive, self-centred men like my father.

In 2007, Brendan and his wife Kerry gave birth to my first grandchild, a beautiful little girl called Ruby who I babysit for at every opportunity. At her christening I got to read a poem, which was such a special moment.

Thomas and his girlfriend Estelle allowed me the wonderful experience of witnessing the birth of my second granddaughter, Leah-Marie. I felt so blessed as I cut the cord and welcomed her into the world. They now have a fantastic little boy called Lewis as well, born in early 2009.

I always have spare beds ready for any of them when they drop by, and the house is full of toys and baby equipment and all the things that were missing from my own childhood. I love to watch the way the girls trust and love their daddies as I was never able to do, and to see their innocence and beauty.

All of us spent Christmas together in 2008 and it was a glorious mayhem. I bought the girls each handmade rocking horses, something that I had always wanted when I was little, something that seemed to me to epitomise everything magical that childhood should be about.

The year 2008 had been particularly special for me because the book I had been writing for years was published with the title *Daddy's Little Earner*, and it became a bestseller straight away, making me very proud.

But despite my wonderful children and grandchildren, and everything I was achieving at college, even despite the fact that my book was a bestseller, I still found myself battling with depression from time to time, still plagued with bad memories and deep-rooted fears, constantly asking myself what life was actually all about, still feeling as if I had failed because of all the mistakes I had made in the past. Marion had taught me to believe in God and it was through prayer that I felt I had been led to write the book, but I couldn't work out what God wanted me to do next.

In the summer of 2008, I went to the Latitude music festival in Suffolk with my friend Polly from college, and there we met some guys with whom we stayed in touch on Facebook. One of them was called James Knight and he invited me to his church. Although I had never found church services easy, I took up the invitation and found myself sitting in a warm, friendly room, crying like a baby, feeling guilty and wretched about my life. Seeing my distress, James comforted and advised me and took me under his wing. We continued to communicate regularly via email over the coming months and he introduced me to a group of his friends through the church and other connect groups. It felt as though for the first time I was meeting people who wanted to get to know me with no ulterior motive; they just wanted to share their friendship.

I began to feel a transformation taking place inside me, an acceptance that God did love me and had always been there for me. The feelings of guilt, insecurity and worthlessness disappeared and I felt as though I had finally come home, that I could forget about everything Mum and Dad had done to me because God was my real parent and the past didn't matter any more.

As I became more confident I began to wonder whether loving God would be enough and whether I could be happy without having a man to love me in the way I had always craved. Then I learned to let that fear go, deciding that if God had that route planned for me He would show me Himself when the time came.

Over the next few months I found myself getting closer and closer to James, a gentle giant of a man at six foot seven inches tall. He is a kind man who treats me with total respect and very gradually we realised we were falling for each other and started dating. The relationship feels healthier than any I have had before because it isn't based on neediness. I had learned that I could look after myself without a man, and that's when it became possible to have an equal, mutually supportive partnership. What's more, as a committed Christian, James doesn't believe in sex before marriage, so it's nice finally to be with someone who loves me enough to see me as more than just a sex object. After everything I have been through, it feels like a miracle that such a thing could still happen to me and I'm overcome with gratitude.

Almost every day it seems as though small miracles are happening around me. Everything in my life has become clearer. I gave up smoking and drinking without any difficulty. It was as if a light had been switched on inside my head after many years of groping around in the dark. My relationships have become easier, college has become more enjoyable and the whole world looks different. I wake up smiling every morning because I know that I am truly loved, and that at last I have truly escaped from the shadow of my father.

Epilogue

At the time of writing this book, I haven't seen Dad for about three years. Last time I saw him I was on my way home from work on the bus and spotted him through the window, sitting at a bus stop. The bus driver switched off the engine and obviously wasn't going anywhere for a while so I got out to speak to Dad, even though I was shaking with nerves. I felt I had to face him, to prove to myself that he couldn't hurt me any more.

He looked older than his sixty-five years, with rapidly thinning hair and far too much weight on his big frame. In response to my questions, he told me he was living in a village outside Norwich.

'Everyone hates me there,' he said, grinning as if he was proud that he could still stir things up. 'Just had to do a course of community service for an altercation with a neighbour.'

He has enough money for his drink now with his pension and everything, so he doesn't need to pimp any more as far as I know. I've heard on the grapevine that he makes a bit on the side selling porn movies, but he didn't mention that. He still seemed full of his own importance, convinced of his superiority to other mortals who work for a living and take out mortgages.

As he boasted and bragged, I looked at the bald patches on his scalp, the huge belly and the reddened face of a habitual drinker, and he seemed totally pathetic and unimportant to me – just an old man who failed to make anything of his life and did so much damage that he has totally alienated his entire family.

He rang me in 2008 after *Daddy's Little Earner* was published, telling me he was going to sue me – although it seemed he hadn't even read the book.

'Did you write about my childhood?' he wanted to know. 'Did you explain why I'm the way I am? Did you tell the truth about what your mother did to me?'

I waited for a lawyer's letter to appear but none did so it seemed he had lost interest in the idea of suing.

He rang me one more time after that, at Christmas 2008, but he was too drunk and rambling to be able to make any sense so I hung up on him.

In the past I would have been distressed to have any contact with him at all but this time I wasn't in the least bit perturbed. From where I stood he was just a sad old alcoholic.

Christians are supposed to forgive our enemies and sometimes I think about trying to forgive Dad, but it's difficult. It's still a step too far for me. I don't feel angry with him any more. I've let all the anger out, which is good because it was harming me to carry it around. I feel disdain for him, I suppose. None of it matters any more because I've made my own life a success. I have overcome the damaging lessons of a horrific childhood and created my own very happy family, the one thing I always wanted. At last I can truly say that I have escaped from my dad.

Acknowledgements

I t would have been impossible for me to have embarked on my healing journey and become the person I am today without the help and support of some very special friends and family.

Particular thanks to Mr and Mrs Davison from Break, Mr and Mrs McQuarrie from Bramerton and those members of the care system who did try to help.

Enormous thanks to Marion Godwin and the organisation Adult Survivors of Incest and Sexual Abuse. Marion, you are a true angel.

Heartfelt thanks to James Knight and all my friends at Proclaimers.

To my special friends who have been there through the good and the bad, the tears and the tantrums – thank you for believing in me: Leigh and Steve, Nikki and Martyn, Auntie B and John, Sandra and David, Lorrayne, Mandy, my solicitor Sandra who fought many battles for me through the courts, Terry Lowe for fighting my corner, and Dan who finally taught me how to take better care of my body.

Eternal love and thanks to my brothers Terry, Chris and Adam and to their families, who bring so much joy to my life.

Thank you to all at HarperCollins who showed remarkable sensitivity and support through the process of writing and publishing *Daddy's Little Earner* and *Escaping Daddy*.

A massive thank you to Andrew Crofts without whom none of this would have happened. You made my dream come true, Andrew – thank you for everything.

And to my sons, Brendan and Thomas: you have been my greatest motivation and inspiration. Lots of love to you and your beautiful families always.